SELECTIONS FROM THE

William Faulkner Collection

OF

Louis Daniel Brodsky

A Descriptive Catalogue

1   Pen and ink drawing by Faulkner, ca. 1918

SELECTIONS FROM THE

William Faulkner Collection

OF

Louis Daniel Brodsky

A Descriptive Catalogue

Robert W. Hamblin & Louis Daniel Brodsky

Published for Southeast Missouri State University and
the Bibliographical Society of the University of Virginia by the
UNIVERSITY PRESS OF VIRGINIA
CHARLOTTESVILLE

THE UNIVERSITY PRESS OF VIRGINIA

Copyright © 1979 by Louis Daniel Brodsky

First published 1979

Library of Congress Cataloging in Publication Data
Hamblin, Robert W
  Selections from the William Faulkner collection
of Louis Daniel Brodsky.
  Includes index.
  1. Faulkner, William, 1897–1962—Archives.
2. Brodsky, Louis Daniel—Library. I. Brodsky,
Louis Daniel, joint author. II. Southeast Missouri
State University. III. Virginia. University.
Bibliographical Society. IV. Title.
PS3511.A86Z7844   016.813'5'2   79-15031
ISBN 0-8139-0830-2

Printed in the United States of America

PS
3511
A86
Z7844

From L. D.
TO MRS. LOUIS HENRY COHN
"Margie"

who instilled in me a love of
and a devotion to
book collecting

in return for which I have given her
my love and my devotion

CONTENTS

Foreword, *by Fred B. Goodwin*	xi
Preface, *by Robert W. Hamblin*	xiii
Introduction, *by Louis Daniel Brodsky*	xvii
I THE PROTOTYPE: *Colonel W. C. Falkner*, 1825–1889	1
II THE EARLY YEARS: *Artist and Poet*, 1897–1925	13
III THE MIDDLE YEARS: *Fictionist*, 1926–1944	47
IV THE LATE YEARS: *Laureate*, 1945–1962	97
V BEYOND: 1962—	149
Index of Faulkner Works	165
Index of Names	168

ILLUSTRATIONS

1	Pen and ink drawing by Faulkner, ca. 1918	frontispiece
2	W. C. Falkner, ca. 1889	2
3	Page of ledger of Ripley Railroad Company	6
4	Page of ledger of Ripley Railroad Company	7
5	Dedication of *Rapid Ramblings in Europe*	10
6	Oxford Graded School, 1908	14
7	Drawing by Faulkner for 1913 Eleventh Grade Yearbook	18
8	Drawing by Faulkner for 1913 Eleventh Grade Yearbook	19
9	Drawing by Faulkner, ca. 1916	24
10	Typescript of early, unpublished poem by Faulkner	27
11	Drawing by Faulkner, ca. 1918	29
12	Drawing by Faulkner, ca. 1918	29
13	Early holograph version of opening of "The Lilacs"	30
14	Leaf from burned hand-lettered booklet, "The Lilacs"	33
15	Leaf from burned hand-lettered booklet, "The Lilacs"	34
16	Burned holograph fragment of unidentified poem by Faulkner	36
17	Burned typescript fragment of unidentified poem by Faulkner	37
18	Typescript of early version of "Mississippi Hills: My Epitaph"	42
19	*The Marble Faun*	45
20	Telegrams announcing birth and death of Faulkner's first child	48
21	Letter from Phil Stone to E. Byrne Hackett concerning *The Marble Faun*	64
22	Cover of *Salmagundi*	70
23	Cofield photograph of Faulkner	73
24	Inscription in *A Green Bough*	75
25	Title page of *Mississippi Verse*	79
26	Faulkner's drawing of Santa Monica, California, residence, 1936	83
27	Page of Faulkner's 1940 will, with revisions made in 1951	88
28	Page 1 of typescript version of *The Hamlet*	89
29	Title page of *The Portable Faulkner*	98

Illustrations

30	Provenance paper for Malcolm Cowley's personal copy of *The Portable Faulkner*	101
31	Half title page of *The Sound and the Fury*	103
32	Page 1 of typescript version of *The Wishing Tree*	108
33	Envelope and cover wrapper for Faulkner's 1951 will	114
34	Page of Faulkner's 1951 will	115
35	Faulkner's inscription to Phil Stone in *The Hamlet*	136
36	Faulkner's inscription to Phil Stone in *The Town*	137
37	Faulkner's inscription to Phil Stone in *The Mansion*	138
38	Dedication page of *The Town*	139
39	"Store Closing" broadside, signed by Phil Stone	147

FOREWORD

Works of scholarship, many of them, emerge from the industry of one person working alone. This particular catalogue, however, developed from an intense but pleasant collaboration of people and institutions, all willing to make special contributions to what they perceived as a work of literary worth.

Mr. Louis D. Brodsky, businessman and owner of the collection described in this catalogue, spent some twenty years sensitively gathering manuscripts, inscribed first editions, private papers, and other rare pieces of material that marked the career of William Faulkner. Professor Robert Hamblin not only recognized the quality of Mr. Brodsky's effort but was influential in the owner's decision to open a part of his collection to scholarship and was crucial to the catalogue preparation. Southeast Missouri State University cooperated to contribute released time for Dr. Hamblin and, as well, to supply other essential underwriting for significant parts of the project. The Missouri Committee for the Humanities, a state-based arm of the National Endowment for the Humanities, supplied support for an exhibit and special lecture series which this book augments and which were designed to provide scholars and the general public with a fresh view of William Faulkner.

Some continue to argue that public and private agencies meld talents poorly in a joint undertaking such as this one. If there is any soundness in that general statement, it was not evident during our work. The reason, perhaps, is that art belongs to more than artists, critics, collectors, and institutions. Art is the property of us all, so it is particularly gratifying to see this remarkable collection of William Faulkner material prosper under the careful stewardship of a team: a private owner, his teacher-scholar friend, a state public institution, and an affiliate of a federal agency.

The results, we think, are worthwhile to American letters.

> FRED B. GOODWIN, Dean
> College of Humanities
> Southeast Missouri State University
> Cape Girardeau, Missouri

PREFACE

The William Faulkner Collection of Louis Daniel Brodsky is undoubtedly one of the most remarkable single-author collections ever assembled by a private collector. The number of inscribed books alone—some eighty copies (excluding signed, limited editions) autographed by Faulkner—makes the Brodsky Collection unique. But there are other equally impressive materials in the collection: W. C. Falkner's ledger of the Ripley Railroad Company; cartoon drawings produced by Faulkner for a proposed high school class yearbook; holograph and typescript versions of early Faulkner poems, some yet unpublished; burned fragments of Faulkner manuscripts (including the hand-lettered booklet of poems entitled "The Lilacs") salvaged from the ruins of Phil Stone's house following its destruction by fire; typescripts of *The Hamlet* and *The Wishing Tree*, the latter of which is considerably different from the published version; numerous legal documents, including four variant Faulkner wills; carbon typescripts of some two hundred Phil Stone letters relating to Faulkner; and Malcolm Cowley's personal Faulkner books, several of which contain the marginal notations Cowley entered while compiling *The Portable Faulkner*. These are indeed significant materials which represent not only a monumental achievement in the field of book collecting but also a magnificent contribution to Faulkner bibliography and scholarship.

Altogether the Brodsky Collection contains some two thousand Faulkner pieces, only about one-third of which are described in this catalogue. Most of the omitted items (some of the later printings of Faulkner's books, certain paperback and foreign editions, a vast number of critical essays and books devoted to Faulkner's work, and many of the newspaper and magazine articles treating Faulkner's life and career) have been described in previous catalogues and are easily obtainable in many libraries. Thus it seemed advisable in this work to concentrate upon the unique and extraordinary materials and to utilize the available space for somewhat detailed description. This approach accounts for the neglect of many excellent books and articles of Faulkner criticism. Since only a limited number of secondary materials could be included, the works of four critics who rank among the best and most influential of Faulkner scholars—Joseph Blotner, Carvel Collins, Malcolm Cowley, and James Meriwether—have been cited as representative examples of the many fine studies which have contributed to an understanding of Faulkner's work and the recognition of his stature as a major literary figure.

Preface

The organization of the catalogue is essentially chronological. The only exception to such ordering is to be found in the listings of the several Faulkner books, in which cases the subsequent printings and editions are grouped with the first edition. British and French editions, when included, follow the American editions. Throughout the text cross-references have been kept to a minimum, but an index of Faulkner's works and a separate index of names have been provided to assist the reader in locating and relating particular items.

The handling of the Faulkner inscriptions in the various books departs from standard bibliographical form not only to enhance appearance and readability but also hopefully to dramatize the real significance of the inscriptions. Faulkner—at least for much of his career—was most discriminating, even stingy, with regard to his autograph. Moreover, Faulkner generally employed a set pattern in signing his books: entering the presentation on the free front endpaper and his name, the place, and the date—usually neatly aligned—on the title page. It is hoped that the arrangement of these entries in this catalogue captures something of the deliberate care and pride which Faulkner apparently put into his inscriptions.

Any work on Faulkner draws upon a long list of outstanding previous studies, and this catalogue is no exception. James B. Meriwether's *The Literary Career of William Faulkner*, Linton R. Massey's *"Man Working," 1919–1962, William Faulkner: A Catalogue of the William Faulkner Collections at the University of Virginia*, and Joan St. C. Crane and Anne E. H. Freudenberg's *Man Collecting: Manuscripts and Printed Works of William Faulkner in the University of Virginia Library* provided the broad bibliographical base upon which this work in large measure depends. Carl Petersen's *Each in Its Ordered Place: A Faulkner Collector's Notebook* also proved extremely helpful, especially in calling attention to variant Faulkner editions unremarked in earlier catalogues. Keen Butterworth's excellent article, "A Census of Manuscripts and Typescripts of William Faulkner's Poetry," not only provided useful material but also supplied the models for the descriptions of the burned fragments of early Faulkner poems. And, of course, Joseph Blotner's indispensable *Faulkner: A Biography* was always close at hand to furnish essential information and checkpoints.

Several individuals provided crucial assistance in the production of this book. Special thanks go to the following:

To Mrs. Jill Faulkner Summers, William Faulkner's daughter and executrix, for permission to include some of her father's unpublished poems and drawings and to quote from additional materials;

To Mrs. Emily Whitehurst Stone, for permission to quote from the letters of her late husband, Phil Stone;

To Carvel Collins, for permission to quote from his correspondence with Phil Stone;

To Malcolm Cowley, for permission to reproduce his statement of provenance for his personal copy of *The Portable Faulkner* and to quote from other materials;

Preface

To Fredson Bowers, who graciously assisted with the manuscript, secured the sponsorship of the Bibliographical Society of the University of Virginia, and handled the preliminary arrangements for publication;

To Irby B. Cauthen, Jr., Mrs. Mary O. Massey, and others of the Bibliographical Society who assisted in various ways in the production of the catalogue;

To Fred Goodwin, Michael Ford, Henry Sessoms, M. G. Lorberg, and William Petrek of Southeast Missouri State University, who enthusiastically endorsed this project and secured the funding necessary to bring the work to completion;

To Paul Lueders, who produced the excellent photographs for the illustrations in the catalogue; and

To Carl Petersen, who kindly reviewed the manuscript and offered many helpful suggestions.

My greatest personal debt, of course, is to Louis Daniel Brodsky, who has generously shared with me both his remarkable collection and his extensive knowledge of William Faulkner. Not the least of my gratitude is for the mutual respect and close friendship which have evolved from our labors together.

ROBERT W. HAMBLIN

Cape Girardeau, Missouri
April 16, 1979

INTRODUCTION

The seeds of the collection described in this catalogue were first sprinkled into a very modest garden dug by a freshman at Yale University in the spring of 1960; they consisted of a random cluster of first editions handpicked by a generous and understanding bookdealer named Henry Wenning, who could see that the young man had been awestruck by the beauty of books.

Of course, I was the young man. I can still recall the wonder on first ascending to the small, second-floor quarters and being escorted by the polished gray-haired man into the shelf-lined inner sanctum of his profession. Reflecting on the experience later, I was reminded of a child lying on his stomach, surreptitiously lifting the bottom of a circus tent and peering in at the most dazzling stream of sights imaginable. And I can also recall the reason for having initially made my way to that bookshop.

That spring, I was a student in R. W. B. Lewis's course in American Studies. Having read *The Sound and The Fury* with total lack of assimilation, I decided to accept my self-induced challenge to tackle Faulkner's novel head-on. The result was a C-grade term paper, written after two futile attempts to make sense of the novel's four oblique sections. But I was not easily dissuaded. I remember thinking that if any author could so thoroughly absorb me without exhausting his literary possibilities and my patience, he was worthy of my respect and my energy. I determined to know more about William Faulkner and his writing, and one way to get "closer" to him might be through owning his books, even having his signature in some of them.

During the next three years I began to branch out, both in my reading of Faulkner's works and in the purchasing of selected materials suggested by Henry Wenning. By June 1963, the collection, as it could then be properly called, consisted of 200 pieces; and it was good enough to claim a prize in the annual Adrian Van Sinderen Book Contest sponsored by the Yale University Library. It was also during those Yale years that Henry Wenning introduced me to Margie Cohn, owner of the legendary House of Books, Ltd., in New York, who ultimately became my sole source of books from that time until 1974. From Mr. Wenning I had gained my initial appreciation for the aesthetics of books; from Margie Cohn, I would develop a profound love for book collecting.

In 1964 at Washington University in St. Louis, where I was pursuing a Master's degree in English literature, I had the good fortune of becoming acquainted

Introduction

with William Matheson, curator of the Rare Book Department at that institution. He was immediately enthusiastic about the Faulkner group that I had brought with me from Yale and suggested that the university do an elaborate exhibit. With pleasure I acquiesced. The show was so successful that I was asked to repeat it in 1965 at the St. Louis Public Library. Through his respect for my efforts, Bill Matheson had further reinforced my desire to expand the collection.

In 1967 I was graduated with a Master's degree, having completed the requirements by writing a 100-page thesis on animal imagery in three of Faulkner's novels: *The Wild Palms*, *The Bear*, and *As I Lay Dying*. By that time, however, I had become an inactive participant in the book market, since few important new materials were surfacing. Thus the collection lay fallow from 1968 until 1974, at which time I decided to reread much of the Faulkner canon I had loved as a student. I discovered I still felt the same electricity I had experienced on first encounters: Faulkner had stood the test of time with my changing sensibilities.

In 1975, Margie Cohn obtained for me a run of very fine and rare inscribed books that Faulkner had presented to his friend Hubert Starr early in the 1930s when Faulkner was indenturing himself to the movie industry. The appearance of the Starr materials—and my ability to be in the right place at the right time with the right ticket—gave me the encouragement to dream that I might advance the long-dormant collection to a level of "importance."

In that same year, the first significant auction in a decade was held at Swann Galleries; the collection of Miss Mary Killgore was being sold to the highest bidder. Many of her books had been exhibited in the seminal Faulkner exhibit held at Yale University in the summer of 1942. From the Swann auction I obtained my first "Faun" (*The Marble Faun*), a copy of which represents to Faulkner collectors the highest mark of distinction. For this auction I had engaged Margie Cohn to act as my confidante, my go-between, in what proved to be the beginning of a new relationship for us: that of bidder/buyer.

Having gathered what then seemed an impressive grouping, I approached Washington University's Head of the Rare Book Department, Mrs. Holly Hall, with the prospect of doing another exhibit. It was hard to imagine that it had been nearly twelve years since that first show. As enthusiastic as her predecessor had been, Mrs. Hall initiated what became a wonderful exhibit. The neatly organized materials and the beautiful brochure that Holly Hall produced were extraordinarily tasteful. Even Margie Cohn, who flew in especially to view the exhibit, placed her imprimatur on the event.

The most satisfying spin-off from this exhibit was a letter from a man named Vance Carter Broach, of Tulsa, who mentioned that he was a cousin of William Faulkner and that he would like to share his knowledge and insights with me. Out of this contact grew a mutual friendship and the basis for the ultimate transfer of much Faulkneriana, mainly bequeathed him by his and Faulkner's great-aunt, 'Bama McLean.

Introduction

Once again in 1976 Margie and I entered the auction house together. Then in 1977 and 1978 we took on all buyers in the three-part sale of the Jonathan Goodwin collection held in New York at Southeby Parke-Bernet. The special materials coming beneath the gavel on these occasions represented a once-in-a-lifetime opportunity to obtain rarities: among them was a fine group of associationally significant presentation copies from Faulkner to Malcolm Cowley, editor of *The Portable Faulkner*.

By this time my determination and my commitment to develop a "world class" collection were cemented; I had rapidly zeroed in on that illusive "point of no return" and had decided to continue ahead despite the inherent risks.

The risks to which I refer define themselves in this manner. A fine collection is ever the result of obsession—obsession being the vicious circle that whirlpools the brain, demanding nothing short of "completeness," total "drowning" while you tread for your life. The risks involved in successfully holding the obsession intact soon get beyond the Monetary (this is the easiest of the madnesses to resolve, justify, and somehow continue circumventing). The greatest risk is that, in having made the decision that at all costs you must obtain "everything," Impasse and Stalemate will loom up before you without announcing themselves; in other words, the availability of important documents and rare books will simply dematerialize like a mirage midway on your journey toward possessing *the* collection, leaving you stranded in the vast lunar landscape named Mediocrity.

Obviously this whole notion is absurd because "completeness" is a fatuous pursuit; and even if it were not, the date, so far as Faulkner is concerned, is too late. Too much is already "under glass" in repositories. Faulkner himself made it possible for the bulk of his personal manuscripts to be placed on permanent deposit at the University of Virginia Library. Yet, it is undoubtedly this very sense of the absurd that stimulates certain dreamers to engage in the Sisyphean quest. The absurdity most likely provides the greatest source of delight and challenge to the avid collector; to him collecting needs no justification beyond its own tantalizing existence.

Among those Faulkner scholars who have been of inestimable assistance in abetting my obsession are Carvel Collins, Joseph Blotner, James B. Meriwether, and Malcolm Cowley. Professor Collins has made available to me books from his personal library, assistance, and encouragement. Dr. Blotner directed me toward the ultimate acquisition of the Myrtle Ramey papers and the books of Eric "Jim" Devine. Professor Meriwether deserves my great appreciation and gratitude because his initial efforts made possible the purchase of the Phil Stone materials and the books of Malcolm Franklin. Malcolm Cowley, with whom I have visited and continue to have a marvelous correspondence, is a gentleman and a Faulkner devotee of the most distinguished kind. His admiration for my efforts is the reason that his prized memorabilia reside in this collection.

And there is another person I choose to include in this digression into sources

Introduction

of motivation and assistance: Carl Petersen. I believe that the results of his nearly thirty years of Faulkner collecting have probably done more than anything to lift my spirits when I have paused at times to ponder the preposterous absurdity of my whole acquisitive endeavor. When I reflect on what Carl has accomplished as just one person facing the enormous task of creating a serviceable and enlightening bibliography, I realize that it is possible, after all, at least to approximate "completeness."

Now it is 1979, nearly twenty years after the inauspicious planting of the first tiny seeds. I still feel that the metaphor is appropriate, and I am reminded of the exultation and surprise my wife showed when she and I visited the Washington University exhibit together for the first time in 1976. Prior to that occasion, she had merely seen the books on shelves, really only glimpsed their spines. But when she saw each of the books artistically juxtaposed, neatly angled, exposed under full lighting beneath protective glass, with their colorful dust jackets peacock-proud, she exclaimed: "Wow, they're so beautiful—the books—they look like tiny flowers that have just blossomed." Her response had echoed the same surprised, excited awareness I had experienced nearly sixteen years before in New Haven on entering Henry Wenning's shop for the first time.

It is my hope that those who have the opportunity to view this most recent exhibit, as well as those who only have the chance to imagine it vicariously by leafing through this catalogue, will recognize that the harvest from this continual planting is bounteous. My most profound appreciation is extended to Professor Robert Hamblin, who has joined me in the harvesting, row by row by row. His enthusiasm, his expertise, and his friendship have made the task of compiling this catalogue no task at all; rather a memorable interlude, a moment to be recollected in tranquillity.

Finally, it is my deepest concern and wish that when I have ceased my tending, I will be able to say that I did everything possible to make the fruits of my labors available to scholars and collectors, especially to those who have a special love of and respect for the works of the man, the writer, William Faulkner. His talent still seems to me to embody the qualities which make of the intangible essences of the spirit and soul Art that is not merely creative and individual, but capable of sustaining itself by inspiring in others the highest desire to achieve excellence. To him I am indebted most of all.

Louis Daniel Brodsky

Farmington, Missouri
January 16, 1979

I

THE PROTOTYPE

Colonel W. C. Falkner

1825–1889

> People at Ripley talk of him as if he were still alive, up in the hills some place, and might come in at any time. . . . There's nothing left in the old place, the house is gone and the plantation boundaries, nothing left of his work but a statue. But he rode through that country like a living force. I like it better that way.
> —*Faulkner to Robert Cantwell*

2 W. C. Falkner, ca. 1889

I

THE PROTOTYPE: *Colonel W. C. Falkner*

William Faulkner's great-grandfather, Colonel W. C. Falkner (1825–1889), was an ambitious and talented individual who, during the course of a varied and distinguished career, was a jailor, lawyer, soldier, landowner, politician, railroad builder, and author. A principal influence upon the life and work of his Nobel Prize-winning great-grandson, Colonel Falkner is easily recognizable as the prototype for Colonel John Sartoris in such novels as *Sartoris* and *The Unvanquished*.

William Clark Falkner was born somewhere in Tennessee as his family migrated westward, and he spent his formative years in Ste. Genevieve, Missouri, where his parents settled. Sometime about 1840 Falkner moved to north Mississippi to cast his lot with an uncle who resided there. Settling in Ripley, he worked for a time at the local jail, completed a rudimentary education, and began a study of law. Between 1847 and 1861 Falkner fought briefly in the Mexican War, established a family, practiced law, became a prominent landholder and slaveowner, assumed an active role in state politics, and wrote a long narrative poem and a romantic novel. During this period also Falkner became involved in a bizarre and controversial chain of violence which left two men dead by his hand. In the ensuing trials he was acquitted of any wrongdoing, but the scandal and animosity resulting from these incidents continued to hound Falkner for many years.

When Mississippi seceded from the Union in 1861, Falkner helped to raise a company of soldiers to support the cause of the Confederacy. Subsequently he was elected as colonel of a regiment of infantry, thus securing the title he would carry for the rest of his life. Proving to be a valiant, if somewhat foolhardy, soldier, Falkner was commended by General Pierre G. T. Beauregard for valor at Manassas Junction. By 1862, however, Falkner had fallen into disfavor with his troops and was voted out as commander. Disappointed but undaunted, he returned to Mississippi, organized an irregular band of cavalry, and reentered the fray. In 1863, partly because of poor health and partly because of his inability to secure a generalcy, Falkner resigned from the Confederate army. According to family tradition, he spent the remaining war years dealing in contraband secured by running the Union blockade which encircled Memphis.

Following the war Falkner returned to the practice of law, restored his plantation, and then—in 1871—entered upon a venture which would eventually secure his reputation as an entrepreneur. The Mississippi legislature, in an attempt to speed reconstruction through the restoration of railroads, had voted to pay $4,000 per mile to any company which would build a railroad at least twenty-five miles in length. Shortly after this law was passed a charter for the Ripley Railroad Company was issued to W. C. Falkner, R. J. Thurmond, and thirty-five other incorporators. The railroad, which was completed in 1872, extended north from Ripley, Mississippi, to Middleton, Tennessee, where it intersected the Memphis and Charleston road. Colonel Falkner, as president and major subscriber, was the principal figure in the construction and early operation of the Ripley Railroad.

Throughout the next two decades, until his death in 1889, Colonel Falkner was actively involved in the difficult tasks of operating and expanding the railroad and of retaining control of the company. In 1873, when the company failed to qualify for the state subsidy and as a result defaulted on $250,000 worth of bonds, the railroad passed into the hands of a New York holding company. Not until 1877, when R. J. Thurmond gained control of two-thirds of the company's stock by purchasing the defaulted bonds, did the railroad return to local control. Shortly thereafter Colonel Falkner acquired half of Thurmond's interest, and by 1886 he had purchased the remainder of Thurmond's stock. According to local rumor, the two men, who had by this time become bitter enemies and who had submitted an earlier disagreement to arbitration, drew lots to see which partner would sell his stock and leave the company. Thurmond lost, though he would later exact a heavy revenge for his defeat. By 1888, with Colonel Falkner in control of the company, the railroad had been merged with other lines to become the Ship Island, Ripley, and Kentucky Railroad; the line had been extended southward to New Albany and Pontotoc; and plans were underway to link the road with a network of track reaching to the Gulf Coast.

In 1880 Falkner took time out from his various business enterprises to write a melodramatic novel entitled *The White Rose of Memphis*. Originally serialized in a local newspaper, the early chapters proved so popular that a New York publisher decided to bring out the story in book form in 1881. The novel was an instant success, selling out the first printing of 8,000 copies within the first month. Since its first publication the book has gone through thirty-six separate editions, the latest having been published in 1953. Colonel Falkner subsequently wrote two additional books—*The Little Brick Church* and *Rapid Ramblings in Europe*—but his literary reputation is based almost solely on *The White Rose of Memphis*. It was doubtless the success of this book which prompted a young William Faulkner to tell his third-grade teacher, "I want to be a writer like my great-granddaddy."

In 1889 Colonel Falkner stood for election to the Mississippi legislature, apparently in the hope of influencing legislation which would benefit his railroad. Siding with one of Falkner's opponents in a bitter campaign was R. J. Thurmond. On November 5, when it had become apparent that Falkner had

Colonel W. C. Falkner, 1825–1889

won his election bid, Thurmond, in an act culminating many years of frustration and bitterness, assassinated Colonel Falkner on the public square in Ripley. This violent climax to an adventurous and controversial career would later serve as the basis for one of William Faulkner's finest short stories, "An Odor of Verbena."

1 8 7 1 – 1 8 8 7

1 The Ledger of the Ripley Railroad.

One of the most significant items in the Brodsky Collection of Faulkner materials is the handwritten ledger containing the records of meetings of the directors and stockholders of the Ripley Railroad Company from 1871 to 1887. Originally the property of Colonel W. C. Falkner, the president of the company, the ledger was handed down to Alabama Leroy, the Colonel's youngest daughter, who in turn gave the document to her great-nephew, Vance Carter Broach. Brodsky acquired the ledger from Broach.

The minutes of the Ripley Railroad Company occupy seventy-three pages of the 337-page ledger (the first thirteen pages and the final 251 pages are blank). The pages are 12½ by 7½ inches and are watermarked with vertical lines. The cover of the ledger is made of marbleized boards. On a paper label affixed to the spine of the book, which has been repaired with tape, has been printed, in pencil (by Alabama Leroy, one suspects), "Papa." All of the entries in the book have been made in ink.

The ledger contains the record of business transacted by the directors and stockholders of the Ripley Railroad Company on twenty-five separate dates, including eleven in 1872, the year the twenty-six-mile road between Ripley, Mississippi, and Middleton, Tennessee, was completed. The various entries are recorded in the hands of nine different writers, one of whom was R. J. Thurmond (see plate 3), the eventual enemy of Falkner who shot and killed the old Colonel in 1889. Several of the entries have been examined, approved, and signed by Falkner in his role as president of the company; and one set of minutes, recording Thurmond's resignation as trustee of the railroad in 1887, is entirely in Falkner's hand (see plate 4).

Various historians have treated the life and career of Colonel Falkner and the history of the Ripley Railroad, and some have argued that Falkner's role in the construction and operation of the road has been greatly exaggerated. However, none of these writers has had access to the old ledger, which clearly demonstrates (as shown by the following summary of the entries for 1871–1873) that Colonel Falkner was not merely one of several principals but indeed the key figure in the early development of the road.

September 18, 1871
  Meeting of incorporators at Ripley Court House. Falkner named a director, then president; Thurmond elected secretary. Capital stock set at $500,000 with shares at $25.00 each.

after the first day of January 1873, W.C. Falkner, or any person related to him within the degrees aforesaid, shall demand of the Ripley Rail Road Company a Ticket of the description aforesaid it shall be the duty of the Company to issue to the party such Ticket. and if the Company should neglect or refuse for 30 days to issue such Ticket it shall forfeit and pay for each refusal the sum of Five Hundred dollars.

Resolved

By the Stock Holders of the Ripley Rail Road Company that the above Contract be and the same is hereby ratified and confirmed and that the faith of the Ripley Rail Road Company be and the same is hereby solemnly pledged for the faithful performance of the same, and that said Contract shall be spread on the records of the Company and a Copy thereof delivered by the Secretary to W C Falkner, which Copy shall be signed by the Secretary and acknowledged before the Chancery Clerk and shall thenceforth be forever binding on the Company.

Examined and approved
June 3d 1872
W C Falkner
Pres

R J Thurmond
Secretary

3   Page of ledger of Ripley Railroad Company

Be it remembered that at a called meeting of the Stockholders of the Ripley Rail Road Company held at the office of the Company at Ripley in Tippah County Mississippi on the 15th day of January 1887 the following proceedings were had.

Upon motion of W. C. Falkner Lee Hines was unanimously elected Chairman and C. L. Harris Secretary.

Upon motion of C. L. Harris a committee of three was appointed to examine and report the number of shares of the Capital Stock represented in the meeting. The Committee after examination reported 1150 Shares represented which constituted a majority of all the Stock.

R. J. Thurmond who had been lawfully appointed as trustee under and by virtue of the Mortgage, and who had been serving as such trustee for the Bond holders and for the Ripley Rail Road Company tendered his resignation. When the following resolution was offered and unanimously adopted. Whereas R. J. Thurmond trustee under the Mortgage, lawfully appointed, has this day tendered his resignation as such trustee, therefore be it resolved that the resignation of said R. J. Thurmond as such trustee be and the same is hereby accepted and all further notice waived, and that the holders of the bonds be requested to appoint another trustee to serve in stead of R. J. Thurmond. A recess of two hours was then taken.

4 Page of ledger of Ripley Railroad Company

The Prototype

November 9, 1871
Meeting of directors. Falkner instructed to "proceed without delay" to employ a civil engineer and initiate construction of the road. Provisions made for the participation of the citizens of Middleton in the project.

December 4, 1871
Meeting of directors. H. W. Stricklin appointed as trustee for the Ripley Railroad.

December 20, 1871
Meeting of directors. President and civil engineer authorized to let contracts for construction of first six sections of the road. Plan approved for collection of payments by subscribers to the company.

March 25, 1872
Meeting of directors. Falkner reimbursed $1,000 for expenses incurred in Jackson during January, February, and March on behalf of the railroad.

April 22, 1872
Meeting of stockholders. Falkner and Thurmond unanimously elected president and secretary, respectively. Falkner empowered to negotiate contract with Memphis and Charleston Railroad for the completion of construction of the Ripley Railroad. Falkner honored for his services in placing the railroad "on a foundation which insures its completion at an early day" by having the first locomotive on the road, as well as the first station north of Ripley, named after him.

April 23, 1872
Meeting of directors. Approved location of the depot in Ripley.

April 29, 1872
Called meeting of directors. Ratified contract Falkner had executed with Memphis and Charleston Railroad. Authorized Falkner "to sign all Bonds Mortgages Deeds Documents and papers and to do all acts and things which shall be Necessary to carry out said Contract."

June 3, 1872
Meeting of stockholders. Ratified contract Falkner had arranged with Memphis and Charleston Railroad, Southern Railway Security Company, and United States Security Company to obtain iron rails, rolling stock, and equipment for the Ripley Railroad. Accepted pledges for loans from stockholders and approved plan for repayment. Adopted a resolution whereby Falkner, in exchange for a $500.00 contribution to aid in the construction of the road, was granted "a first class passenger Ticket which Ticket shall be good for fifty years" for himself and his family.

September 16, 1872
Meeting of stockholders. Falkner, Thurmond, and eleven others elected directors. Engine named "The Ripley" re-named "The Hardy W. Stricklin," in honor of the company official who had recently died.

September 17, 1872
Meeting of directors. Falkner unanimously elected president and awarded a salary of $4,500 for his past services to the road. Approved policy for passes and discounts.

Colonel W. C. Falkner, 1825–1889

September 30, 1872
Meeting of directors. Named Falkner, Thurmond, and two others to a committee to investigate the possibility of selling or leasing the Ripley Railroad to the Southern Railway Security Company.

October 10, 1872
Meeting of directors. Examined and approved Falkner's handling of $81,968.20 worth of subsidy warrants received from the State of Mississippi.

November 4, 1872
Meeting of directors. Falkner granted $300.00 for his services as president for the months of September and October.

December [2], 1872
Meeting of directors. Approved a salary, retroactive to November 1, of $225.00 per month to Falkner as "president . . . and Genl. Superintendent and Road Master" of the railroad.

January 9, 1873
Meeting of directors. Appointed Southern Railway Security Company as agent to take possession and operate the Ripley Railroad for its stockholders, such action having been necessitated by the default of payment on $250,000 worth of first mortgage bonds held by the Southern Railway Security Company.

January [?], 1873
Meeting of directors. Approved plan whereby Falkner could eventually be reimbursed for "various sums of money advanced by him to liquidate the debts of the Company and to build the Depot at Ripley," as well as for the $600.00 which Falkner "hath this day loaned to the Company . . . to be used in paying off the Laborers the amounts due them."

1882

2 Falkner, W. C. *The Little Brick Church: A Novel*. Philadelphia: J. B. Lippincott & Co[mpany], 1882. First edition.

Gray-green cloth. Gold-stamped lettering on front cover and spine. Edges trimmed and unstained.

Free front endpaper carries book plate of Vance C. Broach. Signed on front flyleaf, in pencil: "Natalie Carter Broach."

1884

3 Falkner, W. C. *Rapid Ramblings in Europe*. Philadelphia: J. B. Lippincott & Co[mpany], 1884. First edition. Variant binding.

Light brown cloth. Gold-stamped lettering on front cover and spine. Edges trimmed and unstained.

Baby Roy.   Effie.

DEDICATION

"DEAR PAPA:

"Do pray hurry home. Mamma is crying her eyes out about you and Effie, and I am so very lonesome without you. Everything looks so sad since you went away. I have thought and thought about you, until I have thought you clear out of my mind, and I can't, to save my life, think how you used to look. Old Duke is fat and sleek, but he has become quite lazy since you left. Mamma and I are well; my big doll got its nose broken clear off. Hoping these few lines will find you enjoying the same blessing, I am your affectionate baby,

"ROY."

This letter, which was written by a little brown-haired lass of nine (the pet of the household), met me at Rome. I don't think she meant to express a wish that the letter would find my nose broken, consequently I inscribe this work to her.

Respectfully,

W. C. FALKNER.

PHILADELPHIA, 1884.

5   Dedication of *Rapid Ramblings in Europe*

Colonel W. C. Falkner, 1825–1889

The dedication of this work (see plate 5) reflects the strong attachment between Colonel Falkner and his youngest daughter, Alabama Leroy, and suggests the avenue of linkage between the old Colonel and the novelist William Faulkner, who was not born until eight years after his great-grandfather's death. "Baby Roy," later 'Bama McLean, became one of Faulkner's dearest relatives, as well as one of his greatest admirers and supporters.

The affection and regard that Faulkner held for his "Aunt 'Bama" were evidenced at every stage of his career. He shared with her the early manuscripts of his poetry. He corresponded with her during his walking tour of Europe. He presented to her inscribed copies of his various books. He named his first child, Alabama, after her. He often visited her in Memphis and just as frequently entertained her in Oxford. According to one family story, only Aunt 'Bama could persuade a reluctant Faulkner to attend the world premiere of his novel-turned-film, *Intruder in the Dust*.

Mrs. McLean reciprocated with genuine love and respect for her young kinsman and with support and encouragement for the artist within. One of the earliest individuals—along with Phil Stone—to recognize Faulkner's budding genius, Mrs. McLean took great interest in her grandnephew's career. Throughout the years she avidly read the books, promoted Faulkner's work among friends and acquaintances, clipped newspaper articles and reviews treating Faulkner and his work, and willingly talked and corresponded with scholars who expressed interest in Faulkner. In short, no one was more pleased with Faulkner's success than his Aunt 'Bama.

Doubtless it was from Mrs. McLean that Faulkner received much of his information concerning the life and career of Colonel Falkner. One can easily picture the youthful Faulkner sitting and listening, like Quentin Compson in *Absalom, Absalom!*, to stories of an earlier time:

> So maybe you will enter the literary profession as so many Southern gentlemen and gentlewomen too are doing now and maybe some day you will remember this and write about it. You will be married then I expect and perhaps your wife will want a new gown or a new chair for the house and you can write this and submit it to the magazines. Perhaps you will even remember kindly then the old woman who made you spend a whole afternoon sitting indoors and listening while she talked about people and events you were fortunate enough to escape yourself when you wanted to be out among young friends of your own age.

Apparently Faulkner, no less than Quentin, was more than willing to stay and hear, especially when the stories concerned his great-grandfather.

Perhaps of greater significance than the facts which Aunt 'Bama communicated to Faulkner was the romantic aura with which she enveloped her father. Only fifteen years old when Colonel Falkner was killed, and having been by all reports his favorite child, Alabama idolized her father and always viewed him as the perfect embodiment of gentlemanly grace and heroic courage. Faulkner the novelist would adopt a more balanced view, recognizing the frailties as well as the strengths in the Colonel's character, but he never completely let go of the romantic image. For Faulkner the old Colonel—and perhaps his daughter 'Bama—was always associated with a fabled, mythic past.

The Prototype

ca. 1 8 8 9

4 Portrait photograph of W. C. Falkner, 5³/₄ by 4 inches. Mounted on cardboard, 6¹/₂ by 4¹/₂ inches, with imprint at bottom which states: "Mora 707 Broadway, N.Y." See plate 2.

This photograph is reproduced in Blotner, *Faulkner: A Biography*, p. 2.

II

THE EARLY YEARS

Artist and Poet

1897–1925

For where is that flesh, what hand holds that blood to shape this dream within me in marble or sound, on canvas or paper, and live? I, too, am but a shapeless lump of moist earth risen from pain, to laugh and strive and weep, knowing no peace until the moisture has gone out of it, and it is once more the original and eternal dust.

—"The Artist"

6 Oxford Graded School, 1908

II

THE EARLY YEARS: *Artist and Poet*

The record of William Faulkner's early years reflects the story of an artist in search of his métier. As a child Faulkner, doubtless encouraged by his mother, preferred drawing to writing. Throughout grade school Faulkner was continually producing sketches of locomotives, cowboys and broncos, guns, and airplanes; and in 1913 he was the logical choice as illustrator for a proposed eleventh grade annual. By 1916, when he produced the first of several drawings to appear in a series of University of Mississippi yearbooks, Faulkner had developed considerably his talent with pen and ink. Typical of his skill—and of his potential as a quality illustrator—are the Aubrey Beardsley–type sketches he included in 1920 in the hand-lettered booklet, *Marionettes*.

But Faulkner by this time had also been swept under the spell of the creative power of words. As he notes in his early essay entitled "Verse Old and Nascent: A Pilgrimage," "At the age of sixteen, I discovered Swinburne. Or rather, Swinburne discovered me, springing from some tortured undergrowth of my adolescence, like a highwayman, making me his slave." There followed, under the direction of a close friend and mentor, Phil Stone, a reading of other poets— Housman, Shakespeare, Shelley, Keats, Robinson, Frost, Aiken, the Imagists, the French Symbolists—and Faulkner's own early experiments with verse. On August 6, 1919, Faulkner's first published poem, "L'Apres-Midi d'un Faune," appeared in *The New Republic*. Other poems followed in *The Mississippian* (the University's newspaper) and *The Double Dealer*.

In December, 1924, Faulkner's first volume of poems, *The Marble Faun*, was published. The book was financed by Phil Stone, who also wrote the preface. Stone would often recount in later years how he and Faulkner promoted publication of the book, received the copies, inscribed some of them, and peddled the books to friends and townspeople as best they could. Outside Oxford, however, the book received little notice, and soon Faulkner would abandon poetry (though not poetic technique) for prose.

1908

5 Photograph of Faulkner and schoolmates, 6 by 8¼ inches; mounted on cardboard 10¼ by 14 inches. Imprint at bottom reads: "Oxford Graded School / R. L. Harris, Supt. / 1908 / Oxford, Miss."

Copy belonged to Myrtle Ramey, a member of the class. On verso, in Miss Ramey's hand, in pencil, are listed the names of the pupils and the date "1920—July." Faulkner, identified as "Count Falkner," appears in the second row, second from left. See plate 6.

1 9 0 9

6   Photograph of Faulkner and schoolmates, postcard, 3½ by 5½ inches.

Copy belonged to Myrtle Ramey. On verso, in blue ink, are the names of the pupils and the notation, "From Miss Robbie Eades." Figure in top row, sixth from left, is identified as "William Faulkner."

ca. 1 9 1 0

7   Portrait photograph of Myrtle Elizabeth Ramey, 7 by 5 inches.

Typed notation on verso: "Return photo / to W. M. Reed, / Oxford, Miss."

1 9 1 3

8   Eleventh Grade Yearbook Drawings.

As a junior at Oxford High School, Faulkner completed ten cartoons with pen and ink to be used as illustrations for a proposed class yearbook. The drawings were produced on four 8-by-5-inch sheets of plain white paper, with one leaf containing sketches on both recto and verso. The artwork is noticeably amateurish, but the selection of subject and the assigned captions reflect a keen mind and an impressive sense of humor. Plans for the yearbook were eventually abandoned, and the cartoons were never published. Faulkner subsequently gave the sketches to his friend and classmate, Myrtle Ramey.

The drawings are arranged on the four sheets as follows:

1 leaf (recto: sketches **a** and **b**; verso: sketches **c**, **d**, and **e**)

a. Drawing, 2 by 5 inches. Speeding auto, with "11 GRADE" written on the side, headed toward an arched gate labeled (in reversed letters) "SUCCESS." Dust cloud in rear forms "FAIL[URE]" in block letters. No caption. Signed "F." Upper right-hand corner is torn away.

b. Drawing, 5 by 6 inches. Lineup of five teachers, four holding signs which designate their subject areas as "AGRICULTURE," "ENGLISH," "MATH," and "LATIN." The other figure, apparently the principal [G. G. Hurst], is labeled "THE WHOLE SHOW." Caption, printed in Faulkner's hand: "DE FACULTY." Unsigned.

c. Drawing, 3½ by 5 inches. Figure in cap and gown pushing to the rear four childhood toys—a small horse on wheels, a ball, a soldier, and a top—and facing toward some books. Caption, printed in Faulkner's hand: "WE HAVE PUT AWAY CHILDISH / THINGS." Signed "F." Upper left-hand corner is torn away.

d. Drawing, 4½ by 2 inches. Seated figure, smiling and winking, wearing a top hat and a basketball uniform with "O H S" [Oxford High School] across front of jersey. Caption, printed in Faulkner's hand: "BASKET BALL / CHAMPIONS OF / C.M.A.A. / [rule] / 1913." Signed "F."

e. Drawing, 2½ by 4 inches. Bus loaded with students and driven by a teacher [G. G. Hurst] wearing goggles. On side of bus is written: "ELEVENTH GRADE / SPECIAL. / CONDUC[TOR] G. G. HURST / CLAS[S] OF '13." Road sign in foreground points to "KNOWLEDGE" and "SUCCESS." One figure is shown diving from the bus and another is clinging to the back of the vehicle by his fingertips. No caption. Unsigned.

1 leaf (recto: sketches f and g; verso: blank)

f. Drawing, 3½ by 5 inches. Figure asleep in armchair with lamp and books on table beside him. Caption, printed in Faulkner's hand: "BURNING THE MIDNIGHT OIL ———" Signed "F."

g. Drawing, 4½ by 5 inches. Bearded figure with mug in left hand removing the top from a hogshead labeled "KNOWLEDGE." Caption, printed in Faulkner's hand: "BY GUM, THAT 'AR 'LEVENTH GRADE NEVER / LEFT NARY DRAP IN TH' KAIG!" Signed "F." See plate 7.

1 leaf (recto: sketches h and i; verso: blank)

h. Drawing, 5 by 3½ inches. Stern-looking teacher [G. G. Hurst] sitting at desk on raised platform, aiming a cannon at quaking student seated below. Teacher holds bunch of switches in right hand. Knife, tomahawk, and pistol hang from ceiling. Skull and crossbones in lower right-hand corner. Caption, printed in Faulkner's hand: "THIS IS HOW HE LOOKS TO US." Unsigned.

i. Drawing, 5 by 4½ inches. Teacher pouring liquid from a large container labeled "KNOWLEDGE" into a funnel placed on top of a student's head. On shelf in background are mortar and pestle and stoppered bottles of "LATIN" and "MATH." Caption, printed in Faulkner's hand: "TAKING HIS MEDIC[I]NE." Signed, in artistic script, "WFalkner."

1 leaf (recto: sketch j; verso: blank)

j. Drawing, 5 by 8 inches. Female teacher [Ella Wright] preparing to grind out punishment from "DEMERIT MILL" for fierce, bearded figure standing beside her. Culprit has "A. LINCOLN" printed across his chest. At Lincoln's feet, in miniature, a bully holding aloft a Union flag and brandishing a knife is attacking a much smaller figure holding a Confederate flag. Caption, printed in Faulkner's hand: "THEM'S MY SENTIMENTS." Signed, in artistic script, "WFalkner." See plate 8.

"BY GUM, THAT 'AR 'LEVENTH GRADE NEVER LEFT NARY DRAP IN TH' KAIG!"

7   Drawing by Faulkner for 1913 Eleventh Grade Yearbook

1914 – 1924

9   Phil Stone's Library: Some Survivors.

    Much of William Faulkner's early reading was done under Phil Stone's influence and in books borrowed from Stone's personal library. Years later Stone recollected that, in the summer of 1914, Faulkner "was painting some then and was faintly interested in writing verse. I gave him books to read—Swinburne, Keats and a number of the then moderns, such as Conrad Aiken and the Imagists in verse and Sherwood Anderson and the others in prose" (*The Oxford Eagle*, November 16, 1950). John Faulkner, too, has recalled Stone's influence upon William during this period: "The Stones had a big old Studebaker touring car, a

8 Drawing by Faulkner for 1913 Eleventh Grade Yearbook

seven-passenger affair. Phil loaded it with books for Bill to read and turned the car over to him. Bill would go out on some country road, a side road where it was quiet, and park the car and spend the day reading" (*My Brother Bill*, p. 130).

As Joseph Blotner has noted, Stone was well equipped to be Faulkner's mentor. Having just returned from a year at Yale in which he had completed his second B.A. degree, Stone possessed an enthusiasm for literature bordering on euphoria and a missionary zeal to share his knowledge with friends and protégés. The seventeen-year-old Billy Falkner was not the only person to benefit from Stone's direction. Katrina Carter, a young lady with whom Stone was romantically involved during these years, was a frequent recipient of presentation copies of books Stone admired. When Katrina left Oxford about 1925, she returned many of these books to Stone. The copies Stone gave Katrina provide a further index to Stone's reading tastes at the time when he was the leading literary influence upon William Faulkner.

Many of Stone's books were destroyed in a house fire in 1942; but fortunately some survived, including two titles of particular interest: James Branch Cabell's *Jurgen* and Aldous Huxley's *Antic Hay*, both of which Faulkner inscribed to Stone as Christmas gifts in 1923.

The list provided below, which is arranged chronologically according to date of inscription, supplements the listing of book purchases and orders by Stone compiled by James B. Meriwether and published as an appendix to Blotner's *William Faulkner's Library*, pp. 123–127.

a. Quiller-Couch, Arthur, ed. *The Oxford Book of English Verse: 1250–1900*. Oxford: Clarendon Press, 1912.

Copy used by Stone as an undergraduate student at Yale University. Inscribed on free front endpaper, in black ink: "Phil Stone / Phil Stone / Yale 1914. / English C 35 / English Lyrical / Poetry." Also inscribed on half title page, in black ink: "Phil Stone / Phil Stone."

This anthology includes many of the poems identified by Cleanth Brooks (*William Faulkner: Toward Yoknapatawpha and Beyond*, pp. 346–354) as sources for some of Faulkner's literary borrowings.

b. *Some Imagist Poets: An Anthology*. Boston and New York: Houghton Mifflin Company, 1915. First edition, first printing.

The original green paper wrappers on this copy have been partially destroyed; but the book has been rebound, apparently by Faulkner, in gray paper boards with a brown cloth spine. On white paper label affixed to front Faulkner has hand-lettered in India ink: "SOME IMAGIST POETS / 1915." On label on spine, also in India ink, Faulkner has printed: "SOME / IMAGISTS / 1915." The style of the lettering is similar to that used in *Marionettes*.

The book contains a four-page preface in which the contributors discuss their association and outline the principles of imagism. Contributors are Richard Aldington, H. D., John Gould Fletcher, F. S. Flint, D. H. Lawrence, and Amy Lowell.

The book has been heavily underlined and annotated by Stone.

c. Braithwaite, William Stanley, ed. *Anthology of Magazine Verse for 1915*. New York: Gomme & Marshall, 1915. First edition, lacking dust jacket.

Inscribed by Stone, in brown ink, on front paste-down, "11/13/16," and on free front endpaper, "Phil Stone / Phil Stone."

Includes Amy Lowell's "Patterns" and Wallace Stevens' "Peter Quince at the Clavier," both of which have been mentioned by Brooks (*Toward Yoknapatawpha and Beyond*, pp. 349, 27) as possible influences upon Faulkner.

d. West, Rebecca. *Henry James*. New York: Henry Holt and Company, 1916. First edition, first printing, lacking dust jacket.

Inscribed by Stone, in brown ink, on front paste-down, "1/15/17," and on free front endpaper, "Phil Stone / Phil Stone."

Contains numerous underlinings and annotations by Stone, primarily in sections relating to narrative theory.

e. Bell, Clive. *Art*. New York: Frederick A. Stokes Company, [n. d.]. Third edition, first printing, lacking dust jacket.

Inscribed by Stone, in brown ink, on front paste-down, "3/8/17," and on free front endpaper, "Phil Stone / Phil Stone / Phil Stone." Penciled underlinings throughout text.

According to Emily Stone, this book and Willard Huntington Wright's *The Creative Will: Studies in the Philosophy and the Syntax of Aesthetics* were the two most influential books upon Stone's aesthetic theory and the sources of much of the advice Stone communicated to Faulkner.

f. Flaubert, Gustave. *Madame Bovary*. New York: Boni and Liveright, Inc., [n. d.]. Modern Library edition.

Inscribed on free front endpaper, in black ink: "Katrina Carter / 1917."

g. Hardy, Thomas. *A Laodicean: A Story of To-day*. New York and London: Harper & Brothers Publishers, [n. d.].

Presentation copy given by Stone to Katrina Carter. On free front endpaper, in Stone's hand, in brown ink: "7/30/17 / To Sister on her 2(?)(?)!?1st / birthday." Also on free front endpaper, in Miss Carter's hand, in black ink: "Katrina Carter."

h. James, Henry. *The Golden Bowl*. Vol. II. New York: Charles Scribner's Sons, 1904. First edition, first printing, lacking dust jacket.

Inscribed by Stone, in brown ink, on front paste-down, "10/3/17," and on free front endpaper, "Phil Stone. / Phil Stone."

i. *Poems by John Keats*, ed. with introduction by Arlo Bates. Boston and London: Ginn & Company, Publishers, 1896. In Athenaeum Press Series.

This book was used by Stone in grade school during the years 1908–1910; he returned to it often in succeeding years, dating it finally on the free front endpaper, "3/24/19." Signed on front paste-down in youthful hand, "Phill [sic] Stone." Back paste-down has large flowing signature written twice at bottom in what appears to be Stone's hand from ca. 1912–1913, as well as three signings at top apparently coincident with the 1919 date.

Includes numerous underlinings, bracketings, and notations. In margin beside "Ode on a Grecian Urn" Stone has written: "Beautiful in / suggestiveness."

j. Gorky, Maxim. *Creatures That Once Were Men*. New York: Boni and Liveright, Inc., 1918. Trans. J. M. Shirazi and others. Introduction by G. K. Chesterton.

Presentation copy given by Stone to Katrina Carter. On half title page, in black ink: "Love to Sister / Sept. 22, 1919."

k. Brown, Anna Robertson. *What Is Worth While?* New York: Thomas Y. Crowell Company, 1897.

Inscribed (ca. 1920) on front flyleaf by Katrina Carter and on half title page, in black ink: "Phil Stone. / Phil Stone / Phil Stone."

l. Sassoon, Siegfried. *Picture-Show*. New York: E. P. Dutton and Company, 1920. First American edition, first printing, lacking dust jacket.

Presentation copy given by Stone to Katrina Carter. On free front endpaper, in brown ink: "Love to Sister / March, 1920." Michael Millgate and others have cited Faulkner's borrowings from Sassoon.

m. Masefield, John. *King Cole*. New York: The Macmillan Company, 1921. First American edition, first printing, with dust jacket.

Presentation copy given by Stone to Katrina Carter. On free front endpaper, in black ink: "Love to Sister / Christmas 1921."

n. Hergesheimer, Joseph. *San Cristóbal de la Habana*. New York: Alfred A. Knopf, 1920. First edition, first printing, lacking dust jacket.

Presentation copy given by Stone to Katrina Carter. On free front endpaper, in black ink: "Love to Sister / Christmas 1921." Also on free front endpaper, in blue ink: "Phil Stone / Phil Stone / July 1925."

Faulkner reviewed three other novels by Hergesheimer in "Books and Things," *The Mississippian*, December 15, 1922, p. 5.

o. Masefield, John. *The Dream*. New York: The Macmillan Company, 1922. First edition, only printing, with dust jacket.

Number 620 of signed, limited edition of 750 copies.

Inscribed by Stone to Katrina Carter. On free front endpaper, in brown ink: "Love to Sister / Christmas 1922."

p. Cabell, James Branch. *Jurgen: A Comedy of Justice*. New York: Robert W. McBride & Company, 1919. First edition, thirteenth printing (September 1923), lacking dust jacket.

Presentation copy given by Faulkner to Stone. On free front endpaper, in black ink:

From Bill to Phil, Xmas 1923

Also on free front endpaper, in Stone's hand, in black ink: "Phil Stone / Phil Stone."

Several critics, including Carvel Collins and Cleanth Brooks, have cited the influence of *Jurgen* upon Faulkner's work. Brooks (*Toward Yoknapatawpha and Beyond*, pp. 48–50, 364–366) finds echoes of Cabell's novel in *Mayday*, *Soldiers' Pay*, "Carcassonne," *The Wild Palms*, *The Hamlet*, *Go Down, Moses*, and *A Fable*. Faulkner's own personal library, as Joseph Blotner has documented, contained a copy of the eleventh printing of *Jurgen*.

q. Huxley, Aldous. *Antic Hay*. New York: George H. Doran Company, 1923. First American edition, first printing, lacking dust jacket.

Presentation copy given by Faulkner to Stone. On free front endpaper, in black ink:

From Bill to Phil   Xmas 1923

Also on free front endpaper, in Stone's hand, in black ink: "Phil Stone / Phil Stone." Stone's characteristic marginal notations, in pencil, are scattered throughout text.

r. Wylie, Elinor. *Jennifer Lorn: A Sedate Extravaganza*. New York: George H. Doran, 1923.

Presentation copy given to Stone by Katrina Carter. On free front endpaper, in black ink: "With Love from Sister / February 23, 1924." Also on free front endpaper, in Stone's hand, in black ink: "Phil Stone / Phil Stone."

s. Masefield, John. *The Taking of Helen and Other Prose Selections*. New

York: The Macmillan Company, 1924. Revised American edition, first printing, with dust jacket.

Presentation copy given by Stone to Katrina Carter. On free front endpaper, in black ink: "Love to Sister / May 3, 1924."

ca. 1 9 1 6

10 Drawing of man and woman dancing. On leaf 14 by 8½ inches, unwatermarked. Executed in black and white with pen and ink. Signed, in artistic script, "William Faulkner."

This drawing is similar in style to some of those Faulkner produced for the *Ole Miss*; but Ben Wasson, a close associate of Faulkner at the University of Mississippi, dates this sketch earlier than any of the published ones. Given by Faulkner to Myrtle Ramey. See plate 9.

ca. 1 9 1 6 — 1 9 2 1

11 The 'Bama Poems.

Sometime early in his career, probably on different occasions between 1918 and 1921, Faulkner presented to his Aunt 'Bama McLean (see note to item 3) fifteen poems in ribbon typescript. Only seven of the poems were given titles, but seven others were arranged in sequence and assigned Roman numerals "I." through "VII." Most of these poems quite clearly belong to Faulkner's early phase, when Swinburne and Housman were principal influences, and some of them may possibly have been written as early as 1916 or 1917.

In 1942 Robert W. Daniel arranged for the poems in Mrs. McLean's possession to be displayed as a part of the Yale University exhibit of Faulkner books and manuscripts. Following that exhibit, Daniel acquired from Mrs. McLean two of the poems: "Elder Watson in Heaven" and "Pierrot, Sitting Beside the Body of Colombine, Suddenly Sees Himself in a Mirror." In 1978 Louis Brodsky obtained these two poems from Daniel and restored them to the group of which they were originally a part.

Three other poems from the 'Bama group—"Aubade," "Hymn," and "Pastoral"—were acquired by the University of Virginia and are part of the William Faulkner Collections at that institution (see *Man Collecting*, pp. 125–127).

The twelve poems in the Brodsky Collection were typed with a purple ribbon on thirteen sheets of plain white paper, 14 by 8½ inches, and one sheet of plain white paper, 10 by 7¾ inches. Eight of the legal-size leaves display a watermark depicting a replica of the Great Seal of the United States of America. The remaining legal-size sheets and the smaller leaf carry no watermark.

9 Drawing by Faulkner, ca. 1916

The numbered sequence of seven poems, described in **a** through **g** below, occupies four leaves (recto only), 14 by 8½ inches, watermarked, and is arranged as follows:

1 leaf   Poems "I." and "II."
1 leaf   Poem "III." and first two stanzas of "IV."
1 leaf   Remainder of Poem "IV." and all of "V."
1 leaf   Poems "VI." and "VII."

a. "I." First line, "The sun lay long upon the hills." Four quatrains. Revised and published as IX, *A Green Bough*.

b. "II." First line, "When I rose up with morning." Three quatrains. Previously unpublished.

> *When I rose up with morning*
> *I was as brave a lad*
> *As ever broke a furrow*
> *In sunlight garment-clad.*
>
> *I knew that death came after*
> *But he was far away,*
> *And naught save he could hurt me*
> *While I was strong and gay.*
>
> *But now my furrow's ended*
> *And, ah, I know, I know*
> *That naught save breaking furrow*
> *Could e'er half hurt me so.*

c. "III." First line, "Turn again, Dick Whittington." Five quatrains. Previously unpublished.

> *Turn again, Dick Whittington,*
> *Sang voices in a wood;——*
> *We'll not wait to call you thrice*
> *So take your tide at flood.*
>
> *But it was ever the way of youth*
> *To think that Time will wait,*
> *That he may choose his day to climb*
> *The long blue stairs of fate.*
>
> *"When I'm Lord Mayor of London town*
> *—As tomorrow I shall be——*
> *You'll have a golden canopied throne*
> *And a young page at your knee.*
>
> *But that is that, and it will keep:*
> *Tonight let's think of naught.*
> *The world is soft and sweet as sleep,*
> *As though for us 'twas wrought."*
>
> *Turn back, turn back, Dick Whittington!*
> *For we'll not call again.*
> *But young Dick with a maid was lost*
> *Within a twilit lane.*

d. "IV." First line, "When evening shadows grew around." Five quatrains. Altered version published as XI, *A Green Bough*, omits the following lines, stanza two of the original:

> *They clung and kissed in the leafy shade*
> *And life was fine and clear;*
> *A prince and princess, boy and maid —*
> *Let's stop a little here.*

e. "V." First line, "I give the world to love you." Three quatrains. Published in Blotner, *Faulkner: A Biography*, pp. 185–186.

f. "VI." First line, "When I was young and proud and gay." Four quatrains. Slightly revised when published as XIII, *A Green Bough*.

g. "VII." First line, "Green grow the rushes O." Two quatrains. Previously unpublished.

> *Green grow the rushes O*
> *And merry blows the mead;*
> *Now youth his golden penny O*
> *The spending he'll not heed.*
>
> *Brown turn the rushes O*
> *And flowers blow and die;*
> *And never so gay the spending O*
> *He'll cry it by and by.*

The other five poems in the 'Bama group are the following:

h. First line, "The black bird swung in the white rose tree." Three seven-line stanzas, 1 page, 14 by 8½ inches, watermarked. Beneath last line of this poem is note in black ink in Faulkner's hand: "Mrs. Oldham, of Oxford, who has musical talent, is composing music / for this one." Previously unpublished. See plate 10.

i. "An Old Man Says:" Five quatrains, 1 page, 10 by 7¾ inches, unwatermarked. Slightly altered version published as "I Will Not Weep for Youth," *Contempo*, 1 (February 1, 1932), 1, and reprinted in *An Anthology of the Younger Poets* (1932) and *Lillabulero*, 1 (Spring 1967), 28.

j. "Eunice." Seventeen quatrains, 3 pages, 14 by 8½ inches, watermarked. This copy published in *Mississippi Quarterly*, 31 (Summer 1978), 449–452.

k. "Elder Watson in Heaven." Nine quatrains, 2 pages, 14 by 8½ inches, unwatermarked. Satirical poem about hypocritical church elder. Unpublished.

l. "Pierrot, Sitting Beside The Body Of Colombine, suddenly Sees / Himself in a Mirror." Eight stanzas of varying length, 64 lines, 3 pages, 14 by 8½ inches, unwatermarked. Signed in typescript: "William Faulkner." In pencil at bottom of last page, apparently in the hand of 'Bama McLean, is this note: "Written while visiting in the house / of Mr & Mrs Ben F. Wasson / in 1921."

The black bird swung in the white rose tree:
Heigh ho, lads; its going to rain!
Though they tell you 'ware of a maid's soft eye
Lest the heart within you break and die;
But when you're old, ah, then you'll sigh
For sweet is the fruit that's once passed by!
Heigh ho, lads; for its going to rain.

The black bird swung in the white rose tree:
Heigh ho, lassies; its going to rain!
And the maiden's sad whose breast must yearn
Over last year's roses in this year's urn
For the rose that's withered will not return.
An the bridge be aflame? ah, let it burn!
Heigh ho, lassies; for its going to rain.

The black bird swung in the white rose tree:
Heigh ho, youth; its going to rain!
'Tis sad alone in the joyous spring:
When a boy and a maid are as flames that sing
Then they are wise who join and cling,
For when swallow and summer and leaf take wing
Then its heigh ho, youth; for its going to rain!

Mrs. Oldham, of Oxford, who has musical talent, is composing music for this one.

10 Typescript of early, unpublished poem by Faulkner

This poem treats the same situation depicted in the last of Faulkner's illustrations in *Marionettes*. Unpublished.

ca. 1 9 1 8

12 Line drawings, 1 page, 14 by 8½ inches, Hammermill Bond, in pencil and ink.

a. Drawing, 3½ by 2½ inches, in black ink. Pan and nymph. See plate 1.

b. Drawing, 2 by 5 inches, in pencil. World War I biplane (side view). The tail of this aircraft slightly overlaps the sketch of Pan and nymph.

c. Drawing, 2¾ by 7¼ inches, in pencil. World War I biplane. See plate 11.

d. Drawing, 2¼ by 6¾ inches, in pencil. World War I triplane. See plate 12.

On verso of leaf: early draft of opening of "The Lilacs" (see item **13**).

13 ["The Lilacs."] Autograph manuscripts, 5 pages (3 leaves), in pencil. Early drafts, with deletions and revisions, of material which eventually became lines 1–25, 67–78, and 88–98 of poem published as "The Lilacs." Apparently an earlier version than the holograph copy described in *Man Collecting*, pp. 20–23.

a. 1 page, 14 by 8½ inches, Hammermill Bond. Early draft of lines 1–25. Includes numerous revisions and some lines subsequently omitted from printed versions. See plate 13.

On verso of leaf: pencil drawings of three World War I airplanes and ink drawing of Pan and nymph (see item **12**).

b. 2 pages (1 leaf), 11 by 8½ inches, Hammermill Bond, letterhead: "M. C. Falkner / Hardware / Oxford, Miss."

Recto: experimental draft, 16 lines ending with lines 74–78 in published poem. Much of this material omitted from later versions.

Verso: experimental draft, 15 lines beginning "We had been ['raiding over M' *del.*] / Raiding over Mannheim" (lines 67–68 in published poem). Contains lines omitted from later versions.

c. 2 pages (1 leaf), 11 by 8½ inches, Hammermill Bond, letterhead: "M. C. Falkner / Hardware / Oxford, Miss."

Recto: early draft and rewrite of conclusion of poem (lines 88–98).

Verso: still another version, most of which was deleted from published poem, of lines beginning "We had been / Raiding over Mannheim." Also on this page is a portion of a draft of "A Dead Dancer" (see item **14d**).

14 ["A Dead Dancer."] Autograph manuscripts, 4 pages (4 leaves), in pencil

11   Drawing by Faulkner, ca. 1918

12   Drawing by Faulkner, ca. 1918

13   Early holograph version of opening of "The Lilacs"

and ink. Early drafts, including rewrites, of portions of poem which became "A Dead Dancer." Significantly different from version reproduced in *Man Collecting*, p. 124.

    a. 1 page, 14 by 8½ inches, Hammermill Bond, in brown ink with revisions in pencil. Two stanzas beginning "The hurdy-gurdy in the street below" and "She dances now for apocryphal lovers."

    b. 1 page, 14 by 8½ inches, Hammermill Bond, in pencil. Experimental versions of stanza beginning "The long rain wheels across the sad slow sky."

    c. 1 page, 11 by 8½ inches, Hammermill Bond, in pencil on verso of letterhead: "M. C. Falkner / Hardware / Oxford, Miss." Experimental versions of stanza beginning "The long rain wheels across the sky."

    d. 1 page, 11 by 8½ inches, Hammermill Bond, in pencil on verso of letterhead: "M. C. Falkner / Hardware / Oxford, Miss." Experimental versions of stanza beginning "About her now the white mouths of the dead."

On this same leaf, both recto and verso, are portions of a draft of "The Lilacs" (see item **13c**).

1 9 1 9

15 ["L'Apres-Midi d'un Faune."] Holograph fragment, 15 lines, in pencil on torn half-cover (7 by 11 inches) of [*The Saturday Evening Post*, August 31, 1918].

Quite possibly the first draft of the opening stanza of this poem. Markedly different from other known versions, including the autograph and typescript versions at the University of Virginia (*Man Collecting*, pp. 17–19).

16 "L'Apres-Midi d'un Faune."

New Republic, 20 (August 6, 1919), 24.

Faulkner's first known published work. Also appears in *The Mississippian* (October 29, 1919), *Salmagundi,* and *Early Prose and Poetry*.

ca. 1 9 2 0

17 "The Lilacs."

Burned remains of 36-page hand-lettered booklet of poems, with red velvet cover, which Faulkner assembled and presented to Phil Stone. Hand-printed on title page: "THE LILACS / W. FAULKNER." Verso of title page contains dedication to Stone, with a quotation in French (". . . *quand il fait Sombre*") and the date, "Jan. 1 1920." Contains characteristic reversed s's, like those Faulkner used in *Marionettes* and *Mayday*.

Although this booklet has been severely damaged, with roughly the outside half of each page having been burned away by the fire which destroyed Stone's home in 1942, enough remains to identify most of the contents and in some cases to collate portions of the poems with other known versions.

The material in the booklet, now disassembled in order to protect the fragile leaves, was originally ordered by Faulkner as follows:

[1] Title page
[2] Dedication page
[3] Apparently a blank page
[4] Water color of female figure (see plate 14)
[5–14] "The Lilacs." Varies considerably from published versions and from manuscript version described in *Man Collecting*, pp. 21–23.
[15–16] "Cathay." From *The Mississippian*, November 12, 1919, p. 8.
[17] "To a Co-ed." Subsequently published in *Ole Miss*, 24 (1919–1920), 174. See plate 15.
[18] Unidentified poem. Key visible phrase is ". . . pering candles."
[19] "O Atthis" [first line]. Content and form altered significantly when published as XVII, *A Green Bough*.
[20] ". . . Living." Unidentified poem. See plate 15.
[21–23] "L'Apres-Midi d'un Faune." Slightly different from the versions published in the *New Republic*, 20 (August 6, 1919), 24 (item 16) and *The Mississippian*, October 29, 1919, p. 4.
[24–25] "Une Ballade des Femmes Perdues." Published shortly after its appearance here (with slight changes in punctuation) in *The Mississippian*, January 28, 1920, p. 3.
[26] ". . . Bathing." Unidentified poem. Key visible rhymes are *moon-dune*, *gleams-dreams*, and *eyes-thighs*.
[27] "After Fifty Years." From *The Mississippian*, December 10, 1919, p. 4. Booklet version substitutes "straight" for "bound" in line 12.
[28–30] "Sapphics." From *The Mississippian*, November 26, 1919, p. 3. In booklet line 4 ends with a comma and line 8 is unpunctuated.
[31–33] "A Dead Dancer." Radically different from the holograph version reproduced in *Man Collecting*, p. 124. See plate 14.
[34] ". . . Storm." Unidentified poem. Key visible phrases are "whipping hair," "thin garments to the sun," and "Chicago."
[35] Small drawing of nude woman. Black and white, executed with pen and ink.
[36] Apparently a blank endpaper

18   The Stone Fragments.

The Brodsky Collection includes ten partially burned leaves containing holograph and typescript fragments of early Faulkner poems. These fragments, like the damaged "Lilacs" booklet described in item **17**, were salvaged from the ruins of Phil Stone's house following its destruction by fire in 1942.

Three leaves, one of which is dated "April, 1920," apparently come from an

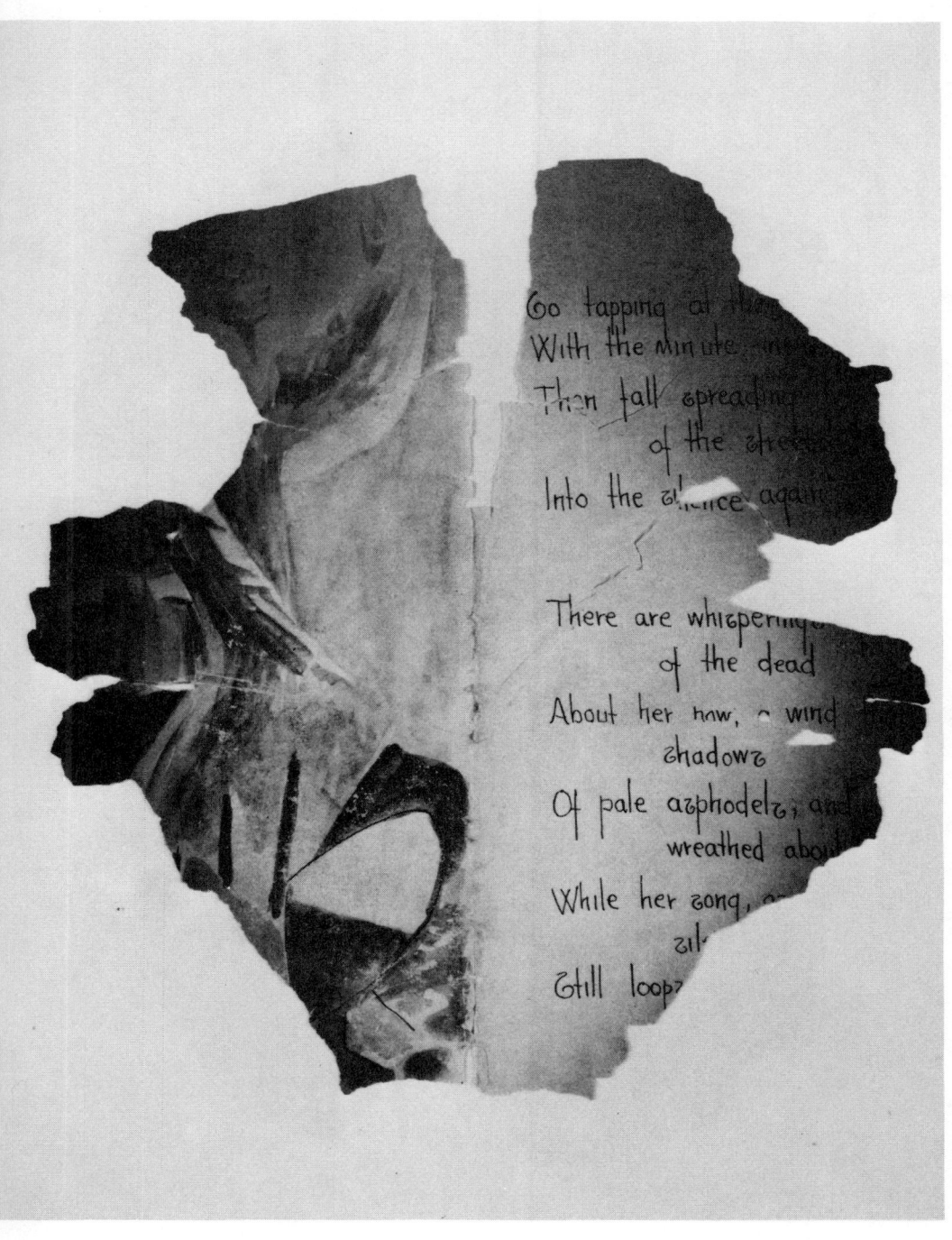

14 Leaf (pages [4] and [33]) from burned hand-lettered booklet, "The Lilacs"

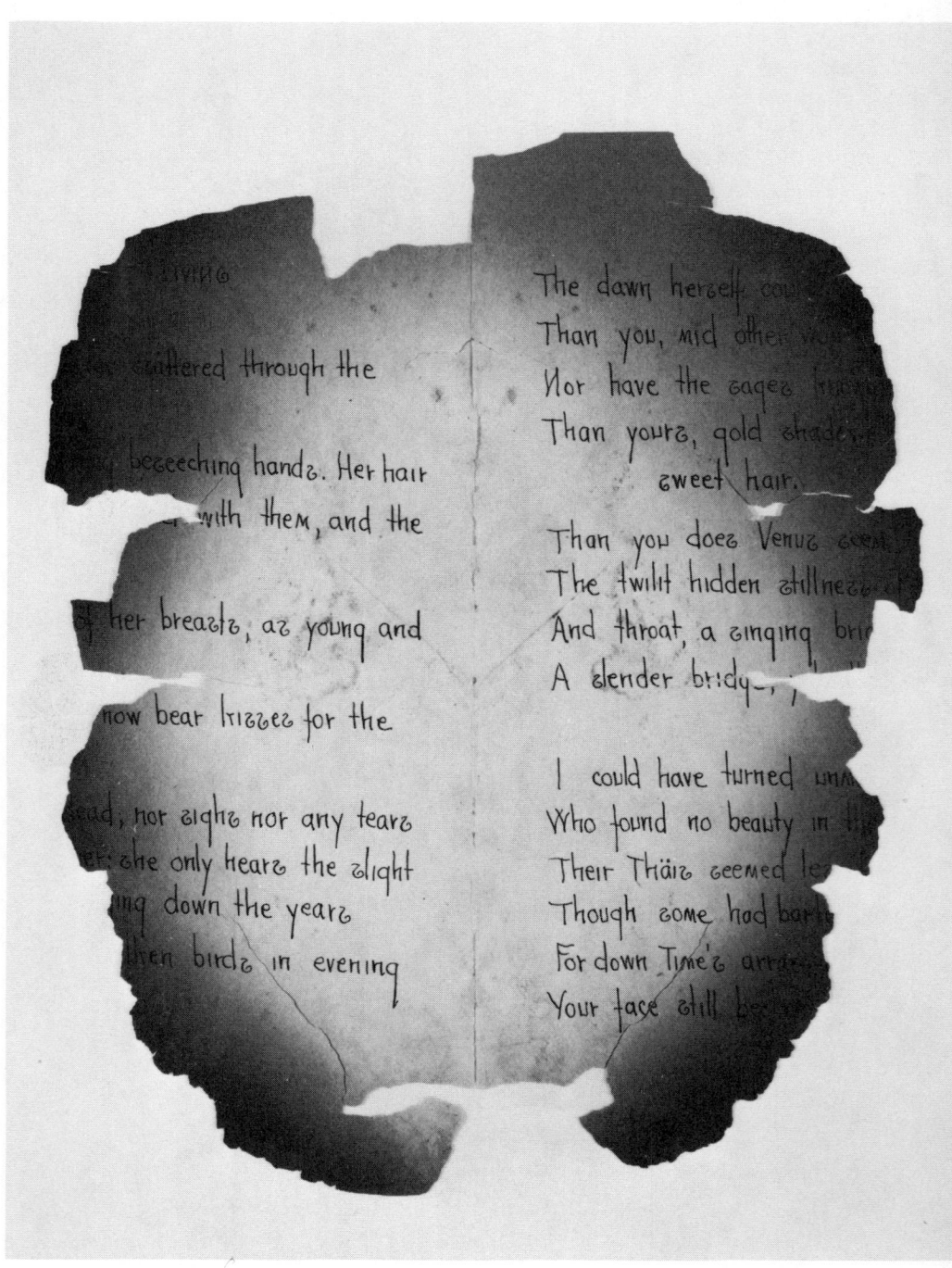

15 Leaf (pages [20] and [17]) from burned hand-lettered booklet, "The Lilacs"

early typescript version of *The Marble Faun*. The other seven leaves contain holograph (recto) and typescript (verso) lines from unidentified poems. In three instances the text of the holograph fragment corresponds with that of a typescript fragment on a different leaf. No watermark is visible on any of the ten sheets.

None of these fragments is duplicated in the Stone papers at the University of Texas at Austin.

a. Burned fragment, 1 page. Ribbon typescript (black ink); 28 visible lines, 22 complete; first complete line, "Below the misted rainbow falls." Description of Naiads in their "cool retreat." Subject matter and wording suggest *The Marble Faun*, although this passage does not appear in published version. Contains two holograph emendations in Faulkner's hand.

b. Burned fragment, 1 page. Ribbon typescript (black ink); 24 visible lines, 19 complete; first complete line, "Above me stand the inky trees." Includes 14-line section beginning "The stream flows calmly without so[und]" and ending "Throbs her sorrow out to them" which appears, in slightly altered form, in *The Marble Faun* (pp. 31–32); but preceding and following lines do not correspond with published version.

c. Burned fragment, 1 page. Ribbon typescript (black ink); 7 visible lines, 3 complete; first complete line, "Her tears are what men call dew." Includes ". . . th things that I would know / . . . ixt . . . above and earth below" (cf. *The Marble Faun*, pp. 12, 49). Apparently the last page of the typescript; typed below last line: "WILLIAM FAULKNER. / April, 1920."

d. Burned fragment, 1 leaf. Recto: autograph manuscript (in pencil); 18 visible lines, 12 complete; first complete line, "It was you who, in a certain dark." Unidentified poem.

Verso: ribbon typescript (purple ink); 18 visible lines, none complete; first line, ". . . rose and leaned its breast upon the horizon." Unidentified poem.

e. Burned fragment, 1 leaf. Recto: autograph manuscript (in pencil); 14 visible lines, none complete; eighth line, ". . . the dark whence all are born." Unidentified poem.

Verso: ribbon typescript (purple ink); 21 visible lines, none complete; sixth line, ". . . heavy mouthed, taking his trembling flesh." Unidentified poem.

f. Burned fragment, 1 leaf. Recto: autograph manuscript (in pencil); 15 visible lines, 11 complete; first complete line, "We hear an untouched music pause and sing." Unidentified poem.

Verso: ribbon typescript (purple ink); 20 visible lines, none complete; eleventh line, ". . . lone trolley thrusts the silence from a street." Roman numeral "XX." appears below last visible line. Unidentified poem with obvious Prufrockian echoes.

g. Burned fragment, 1 leaf. Recto: autograph manuscript (in pencil); 15 visi-

>   ... last beauty
>   ... hand ...
>   ...ed the door had ... her beauty
>   ... who ~~beside her~~ upon her lover
> Silent, softly smiling stood,
> ~~And bad her flowers~~
> And lowered eyed, her glances lightly laid
> Like flowers from a ~~pale quick~~ narrow fugitive hand
>
> And at my cry the enigmatic door
> Swung backward, and the minister bore of claw,
> Stood erect, but at her scarce formed nod
> Sank back and disappeared, and I saw
> My carnate dream wait, slow dies like a flower
> In a casket of doubt I ... ...
> ~~From this~~ Whence in strange white silence the head changed
> ~~And sleeping yet~~, she slowly raised her hand.
>
> And all my life flowed back into my eyes,
> And my mouth grew thin and sharp with pain,
> ... she lightly swayed
> ... ... soft gleamed hair, and all desire,

16 Burned holograph fragment of unidentified poem by Faulkner

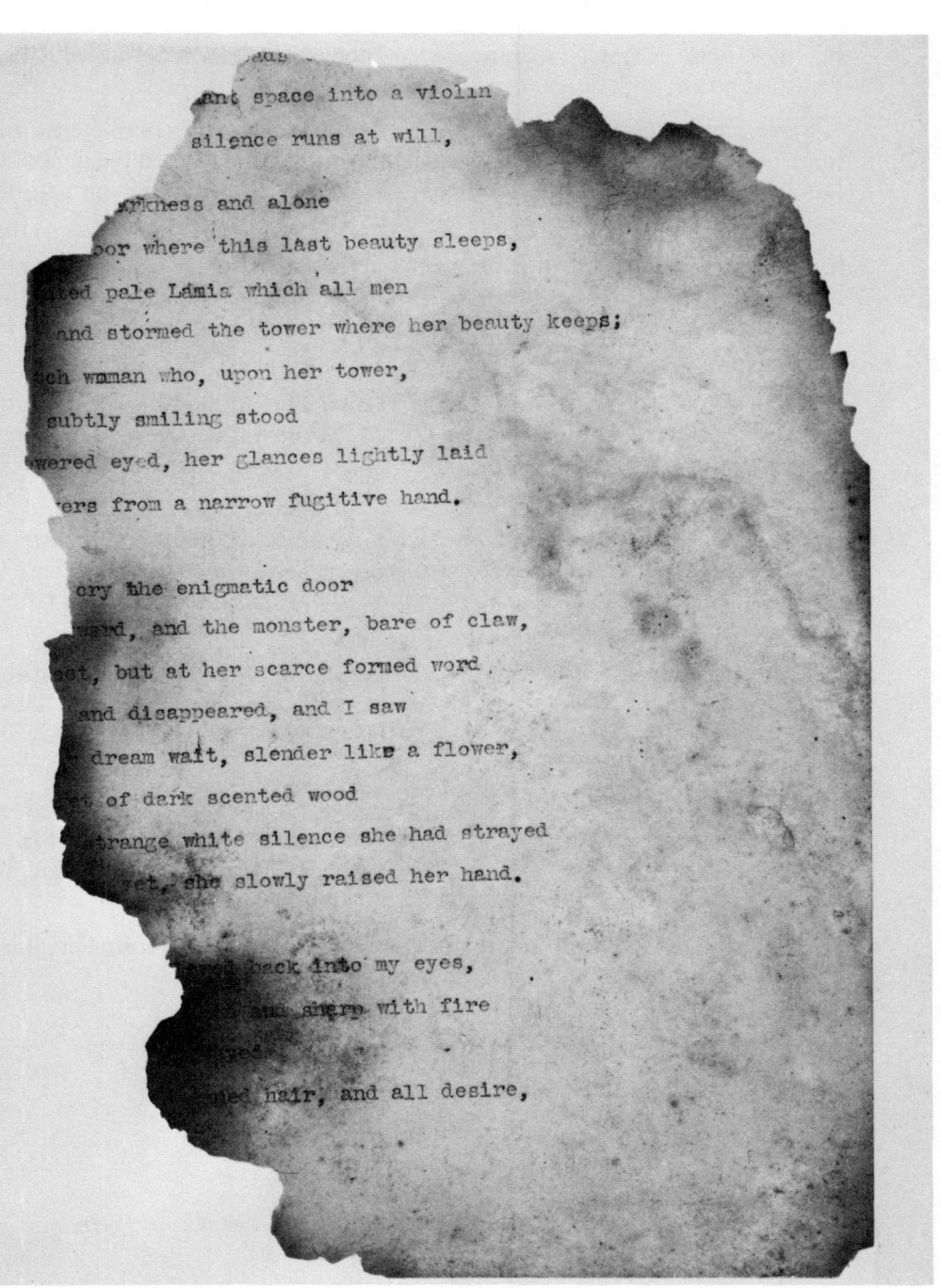

17 Burned typescript fragment of unidentified poem by Faulkner

ble lines, none complete; sixth line, ". . . down past the somber hills." Unidentified poem, with deletions and revisions.

Verso: ribbon typescript (purple ink); 22 visible lines, none complete; ninth line, ". . . owered eyed, her glances lightly laid." Unidentified poem about Lamia. This page of typescript roughly corresponds to the autograph manuscript described in **h** below. See plate 17.

h. Burned fragment, 1 leaf. Recto: autograph manuscript (in pencil); 20 visible lines, 17 complete; seventh line, "And, lowered eyed, her glances lightly laid." Unidentified poem about Lamia. This page of holograph roughly corresponds to the typescript described in **g** above. See plate 16.

Verso: ribbon typescript (purple ink); 24 visible lines, none complete; eighth line, ". . . et us talk of those dark silent days." Unidentified poem. This page of typescript roughly corresponds to the autograph manuscript described in **i** below.

i. Burned fragment, 1 leaf. Recto: autograph manuscript (in pencil); 18 visible lines, 14 complete; third line, ". . . s, let us talk of those dark silent days." Unidentified poem. This page of holograph roughly corresponds to the typescript described in **h** above.

Verso: ribbon typescript (purple ink); 21 visible lines, none complete; fourth line, ". . . er that first strange passionate spring." Unidentified poem. This page of typescript roughly corresponds to the autograph manuscript described in **j** below.

j. Burned fragment, 1 leaf. Recto: autograph manuscript (in pencil); 14 visible lines, 13 complete; sixth line, "Do you remember that ['strange' *del.*] first strange passionate spring." Unidentified poem. This page of holograph roughly corresponds to the typescript described in **i** above.

Verso: ribbon typescript (purple ink); 15 visible lines, none complete; first line, ". . . er the same, always the same." Unidentified poem.

1922

19 "Portrait."

The Double Dealer, 3 (June 1922), 337.

First publication of poem reprinted in *Salmagundi* and *Early Prose and Poetry*.

1924

20 "Verse, Old and Nascent: A Pilgrimage." Carbon typescript, 7 pages, 11 by 8½ inches, unwatermarked onionskin. On last page is the typed notation: "William Faulkner. / Oxford, Mississippi. / October, 1924."

This copy, which Faulkner gave to Myrtle Ramey, is only slightly different from the version of this essay published in *The Double Dealer*, 7 (April 1925), 129–131, and reprinted in *Salmagundi* and *Early Prose and Poetry*.

The collation provided below is keyed to the text in *Early Prose and Poetry*.

Title:	Verse, Old]	Verse Old] EPP
Paragraph 1:	foot-prints]	footprints] EPP
Paragraph 2:	my interest in fornication]	my concupiscence] EPP
Paragraph 3:	accompanyment]	accompaniment] EPP
	stringed]	stringed] EPP
Paragraph 6:	stuff",]	stuff,"] EPP
	know",]	know,"] EPP
Paragraph 8:	paper-bound]	paperbound] EPP
Paragraph 9:	Spencer]	Spenser] EPP
	Nightingale]	nightingale] EPP
	hear",]	hear,"] EPP
Paragraph 10:	cause for interest]	cause of interest] EPP
	Shelly]	Shelley] EPP

21 "Mississippi Poems."

On December 30, 1924, in Phil Stone's law office, Faulkner presented to his friend and former schoolmate, Myrtle Ramey, an inscribed copy of *The Marble Faun* (see item **24**) and a group of twelve poems in carbon typescript. The poems were accompanied by a typed cover sheet, listing the title of the collection, in part or in whole, as "Mississippi Poems" and showing the place and time of composition or compilation as "Oxford, Mississippi. / October, 1924." In holograph Faulkner added to this title page: "Autographed for Myrtle Ramey / 30 day of December, 1924 / William Faulkner."

At the top of each page of typescript, including the title page, Stone had added in his own hand: "Publication rights reserved. Not to be published without the written consent of the author or that of Phil Stone." This note suggests that Faulkner and Stone had previously sent these same poems out to publishers.

The first seven poems in the Ramey group were assigned Roman numerals, whereas the last five are unnumbered. The title page may relate to only the numbered sequence, since four of the additional five poems are dated November or December, rather than October as shown on the cover sheet. Nine of the twelve poems have titles. Each poem carries Faulkner's signature in both typescript and holograph. All thirteen pages of text, as well as the title page, are on unwatermarked onionskin, 11 by 8½ inches.

Nine of the poems presented to Ramey were subsequently published, though in considerably altered (in at least two instances, corrupt) versions. Three of the poems remain unpublished.

a. "I." First line, "Shall I recall this tree, when I am old." Four quatrains, 1 page. Signed in both typescript and holograph: "William Faulkner."

Slightly different version reproduced in *Man Working*, p. 77. The collation which follows is keyed to this text.

line 2: fills] filled] MW
line 3: is bought] was bought] MW
line 6: their purple] to purple] MW
line 9: hushèd] hushed] MW
line 10: tree-tops] tree tops] MW
line 14: wind centaurs] wind-centaurs] MW
line 15: at beauty's] with beauty's] MW

b. "II." First line, "Moon of death, moon of bright despair." Four quatrains, 1 page. Signed in both typescript and holograph: "William Faulkner." Unpublished.

c. "III. / INDIAN SUMMER." Three quatrains and a couplet, 1 page. Signed in both typescript and holograph: "William Faulkner."

Published, with the textual changes noted below, as XXXV, *A Green Bough*. Divided into octave and sestet in published version.

line 2: leaves,] leaves;] AGB
line 4: toward her] of her] AGB
line 9: So, too, the world] Thus the world] AGB
line 11: clean rain . . . Summer's] lean rain . . . summer's] AGB
line 13: Rejoice] rejoice] AGB
line 14: wood-smoke] woodsmoke] AGB

d. "IV. / WILD GEESE." Four quatrains, 1 page. Signed in both typescript and holograph: "William Faulkner."

Published with alterations as "Over the World's Rim," *New Republic*, 74 (April 12, 1933), 253, and as XXVIII, *A Green Bough*. The collation below is keyed to *A Green Bough*.

line 2: cold;] cold:] AGB
line 3: What their lonely voices stir] What do their lonely voices wake] AGB
line 4: This dust ere it was] In this dust ere 'twas] AGB
line 5: sleeping,] sleeping] AGB
line 9: This hand] The hand] AGB
line 11: lonely! Mine] lonely: mine] AGB
line 12: Thine] Then] AGB
line 14: vain!] vain,] AGB
line 16: And] And,] AGB

e. "V." First line, "He furrows the brown earth, doubly sweet." Eight quatrains, 2 pages. Both pages signed in typescript and holograph: "William Faulkner."

Published, with the variations noted below, as VIII, *A Green Bough*.

line 8: And clean its odorous strength about him blown.] And the clean smell of its strength upon him blown.] AGB
line 9: From] Against] AGB
line 11: here] there] AGB
line 13: its hurtling gold] its flashing scut] AGB
line 14: to] in] AGB

line 15: Of fluid fear across the mold.]   Of fright from furrow hill to rut.] AGB
line 16: shouts. The]   shouts: the] AGB
line 17: voice as]   voice, as] AGB
line 18: cool]   brown] AGB
line 19: And then]   Then] AGB
line 20: glossy]   burnished] AGB
line 21: its life]   all life] AGB
line 25: He moves again, to bells of sheep]   Beneath the marbled sky go sheep] AGB
line 27: rumorous]   waking] AGB
line 28: faint-leaved]   faintleaved] AGB
line 29: sleep]   air] AGB
line 31: To a simple heart, for]   With his own sweat, since] AGB
line 32: Might]   May] AGB

f. "VI. / THE POET GOES BLIND." Four five-line stanzas, 1 page. Signed in holograph: "William Faulkner." Signed in typescript: "William Faulkner, / Oxford, Mississippi, / 29 Oct. 1924." Unpublished.

g. "VII. / Mississippi Hills: MY EPITAPH." Four quatrains, 1 page. Signed in both typescript and holograph: "William Faulkner." Typescript title is "MY EPITAPH." Added in Faulkner's hand: "Mississippi Hills:" See plate 18.

This poem published as "My Epitaph" in *Contempo*, 1 (February 1, 1932), 2, and in *An Anthology of the Younger Poets* (1932); considerably revised versions appear as *This Earth* (1932), as XLIV in *A Green Bough*, and as "If There Be Grief" in *Mississippi Verse* (1934).

A different typescript of this poem is reproduced in *Man Working*, p. 76.

h. "THE GALLOWS." Three stanzas of six, eight, and six lines respectively, 1 page. Signed in typescript: "William Faulkner, / Oxford, Mississippi, / 29 Oct. 1924." Signed in holograph: "William Faulkner." Stone's note across top is slightly different from that on others in this group; it reads: "Not to be published without the written consent of the author or of Phil Stone."

Published as XIV, *A Green Bough*. The published version includes three final quatrains not included in this typescript.

i. "PREGNA[N]CY." Four quatrains, 1 page. Signed in both typescript and holograph: "William Faulkner." Also added in typescript: "Oxford, Mississippi / November 10, 1924."

Published, with the changes indicated below, as XXIX, *A Green Bough*.

line 2: wet,]   wet] AGB
line 7: lyre,]   lyre] AGB
line 9: difficence]   difference] AGB
line 11: be recompense]   are recompense] AGB
line 12: unravishèd]   unravished] AGB

Publication rights reserved. Not to be republished without the written consent of the author or that of Phil Stone.

VII.

Mississippi Hills : MY EPITAPH.

Far blue hills, where I have pleasured me,
Where on silver feet in dogwood cover
Spring follows, singing close the bluebird's "Lover!"
When to the road I trod an end I see,

Let this soft mouth, shaped to the rain,
Be but golden grief for grieving's sake,
And these green woods be dreaming here to wake
Within my heart when I return again.

Return I will! Where is there the death
While in these blue hills slumbrous overhead
I'm rooted like a tree? Though I be dead,
This soil that holds me fast will find me breath.

The stricken tree has no young green to weep
The golden years we spend to buy regret.
So let this be my doom, if I forget
That there's still spring to shake and break my sleep.

William Faulkner.
William Faulkner

18   Typescript of early version of "Mississippi Hills: My Epitaph"

line 14: the rain]   soft rain] AGB
line 15: shakes,]   shakes] AGB

j. "NOVEMBER 11TH." Four quatrains, 1 page. Signed in both typescript and holograph: "William Faulkner." Also added in typescript: "Oxford, Mississippi. / November 11, 1924."

Published, with only slight changes in punctuation and capitalization, as "Gray the Day," *New Republic*, 74 (April 12, 1933), 253, and as XXX, *A Green Bough*. Last stanza appears as epigraph for *Soldiers' Pay*.

k. "DECEMBER / TO ELISE." Four quatrains, 1 page. Signed in both typescript and holograph: "William Faulkner." Also added in typescript: "Oxford, Mississippi, / December 10, 1924." Unpublished.

l. "MARCH." Two quatrains and sestet, 1 page. Signed in both typescript and holograph: "William Faulkner." Also added in typescript: "Oxford, Mississippi, / December 15, 1924."

Published as XLII, *A Green Bough*, with which the following collation is keyed. Arranged as octave and sestet in *A Green Bough*.

line 2:   snake's]   Snake's] AGB
line 5:   Through winter's night man can take for warm]   In winter's night man may keep him warm] AGB
line 6:   Forgiveness of old sins he did commit,]   Regretting olden sins he did omit;] AGB
line 8:   that, with birth,]   that with breath] AGB
line 9:   away——]   away,] AGB
line 10: who has]   and has] AGB
line 12: But feeds and fans man's crumb of fire——]   But ever feeds man's crumb of fire,] AGB
line 13: eagle]   swallow] AGB
line 14: Nazarine]   Nazarene] AGB

22 *The Marble Faun*.

Boston: The Four Seas Company, [December 15] 1924.
First edition, only printing, lacking dust jacket.

Portion of spine, free front endpaper, and pages 35–36 are missing.
Inscribed copy. On title page, in brown ink:

> *William Faulkner*
> *19 December 1924*

23 *The Marble Faun*.

Boston: The Four Seas Company, 1924.
First edition, only printing, with dust jacket.

Presentation copy. On free front endpaper, in blue ink:

> *To Joe Parks,*
> *from W Faulkner*

On title page, in blue ink:

> *William Faulkner*
> *Oxford, Miss*
> *24 December 1924*

Joe Parks, an Oxford banker who displaced Faulkner's grandfather, J. W. T. Falkner, as president of the First National Bank of Oxford, was the prototype for Flem Snopes.

24 *The Marble Faun.*

Boston: The Four Seas Company, 1924.
First edition, only printing, with dust jacket.

Presentation copy. One of a small number inscribed by both Faulkner and Phil Stone. See plate 19.
On free front endpaper, in black ink:

> *To Myrtle Ramey, my old friend and school mate.*
> *Bill Faulkner*

On title page, in black ink:

> *William Faulkner*
> *30 December 1924*

Also on free front endpaper, in Stone's hand, in black ink: "A greeting to my old friend Myrtle Ramey / Phil Stone."

25 *The Marble Faun.*

Boston: The Four Seas Company, 1924.
First edition, only printing, lacking dust jacket. Title page carries Fred O'Brien's book stamp.

Presentation copy. On free front endpaper, in brown ink:

> *To Fred O'Brien,*
>   *In memory of old times, before the*
> *South Seas went dry.*
>   *Bill Faulkner*

On title page, in brown ink:

> *William Faulkner*
> *12 May 1925*

1 9 2 5

26 *The Double Dealer*, 7 (January–February 1925).

Contains three items by Faulkner:

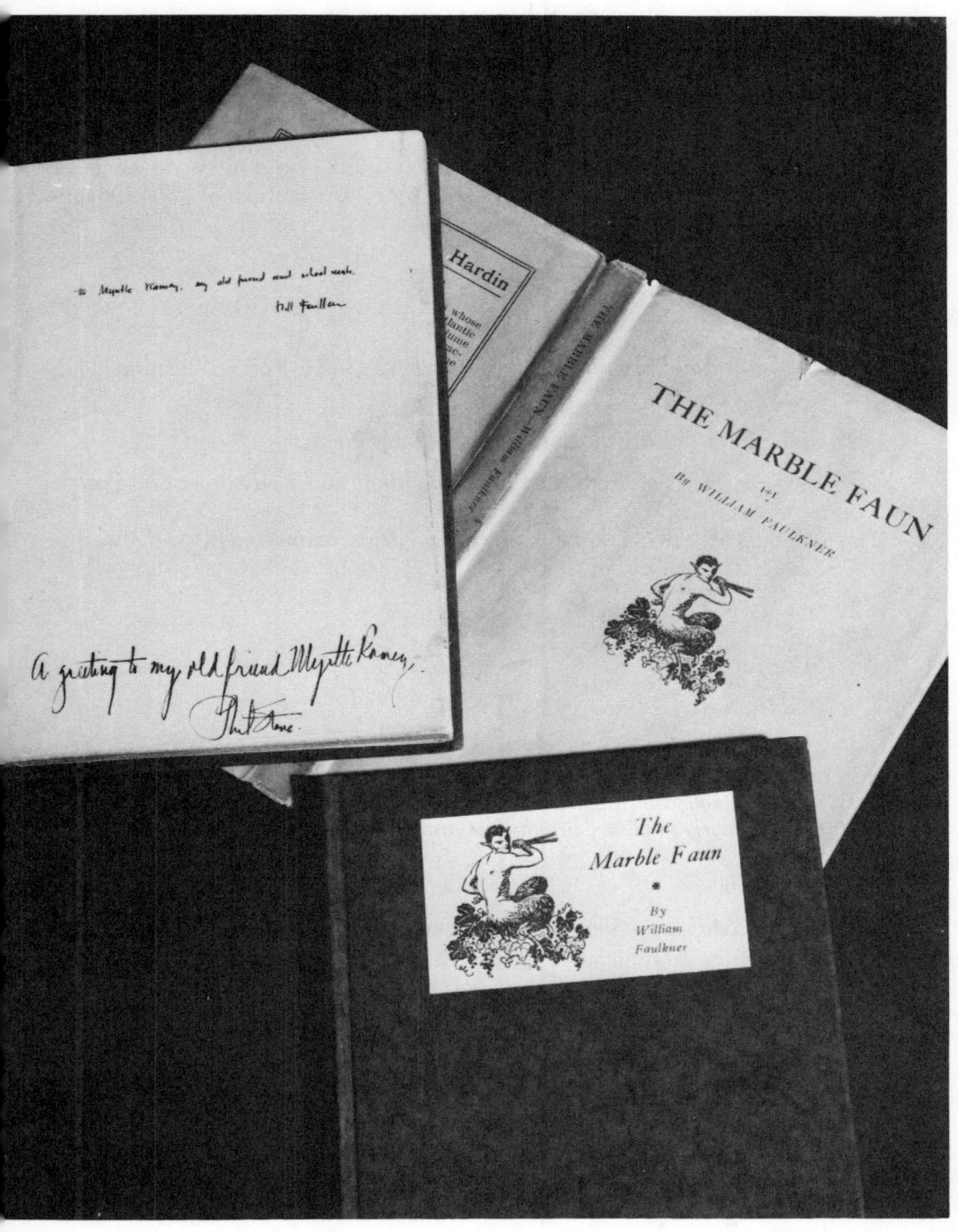

19 *The Marble Faun.* Upper copy inscribed by both Faulkner and Phil Stone to Myrtle Ramey.

    a. "On Criticism," 83–84. First publication of essay reprinted in *Salmagundi* and *Early Prose and Poetry*.

    b. "Dying Gladiator," 85. First publication of poem reprinted in *Salmagundi* and *Early Prose and Poetry*.

    c. "New Orleans," 102–107. First publication of group of eleven prose sketches reprinted in *Salmagundi* and American edition of *New Orleans Sketches*.

27 *The Double Dealer*, 7 (April 1925).

Contains two items by Faulkner:

    a. "Verse Old and Nascent: A Pilgrimage," 129–131. First publication of this essay.

    b. "The Faun," 148. First publication of this poem.

Both of these pieces are reprinted in *Salmagundi* and *Early Prose and Poetry*.

28 Cooper, Monte. "The Book of Verses." *The Commercial Appeal*, April 5, 1925, Sec. III, p. 10.

    Review of *The Marble Faun*.

29 "The Lilacs."

The Double Dealer, 7 (June 1925), 185–187.

    First publication of poem which became I, *A Green Bough*.
"The Lilacs" also appears in *Anthology of Magazine Verse for 1925*, *Salmagundi* (1932), and *Anthology of Magazine Verse for 1958 and Anthology of Poems from the Seventeen Previously Published Braithwaite Anthologies*.

30 "The Lilacs."

Anthology of Magazine Verse for 1925 and Yearbook of American Poetry, ed. William Stanley Braithwaite. Boston: B. J. Brimmer Company, 1925, pp. 115–118. First edition, lacking dust jacket.

31 "Ode To the Louver."

Ribbon typescript (black ink), 2 pages, 11 by 8½ inches, unwatermarked. Humorous poem by Faulkner. Six seven-line stanzas.
    Accompanied by humorous letter, ribbon typescript (black ink), 1 page, 11 by 8½ inches, unwatermarked. Dated "Paris, (France) / November 1st. 1925." Addressed to "Mr. H. Mencken, magazine orthur" and signed in typescript with pseudonym "Ernest V. Simms."

    Faulkner composed these satirical pieces in Paris in 1925 and mailed them home to his friend Phil Stone.
    This copy of poem and letter varies only slightly from the one at the University of Texas at Austin, published in *Mississippi Quarterly*, 27 (Summer 1974), 333–335.

III

THE MIDDLE YEARS

Fictionist

1926–1944

Beginning with *Sartoris* I discovered that my own little postage stamp of native soil was worth writing about and that I would never live long enough to exhaust it, and by sublimating the actual into apocryphal I would have complete liberty to use whatever talent I might have to its absolute top.

—*Interview with Jean Stein*

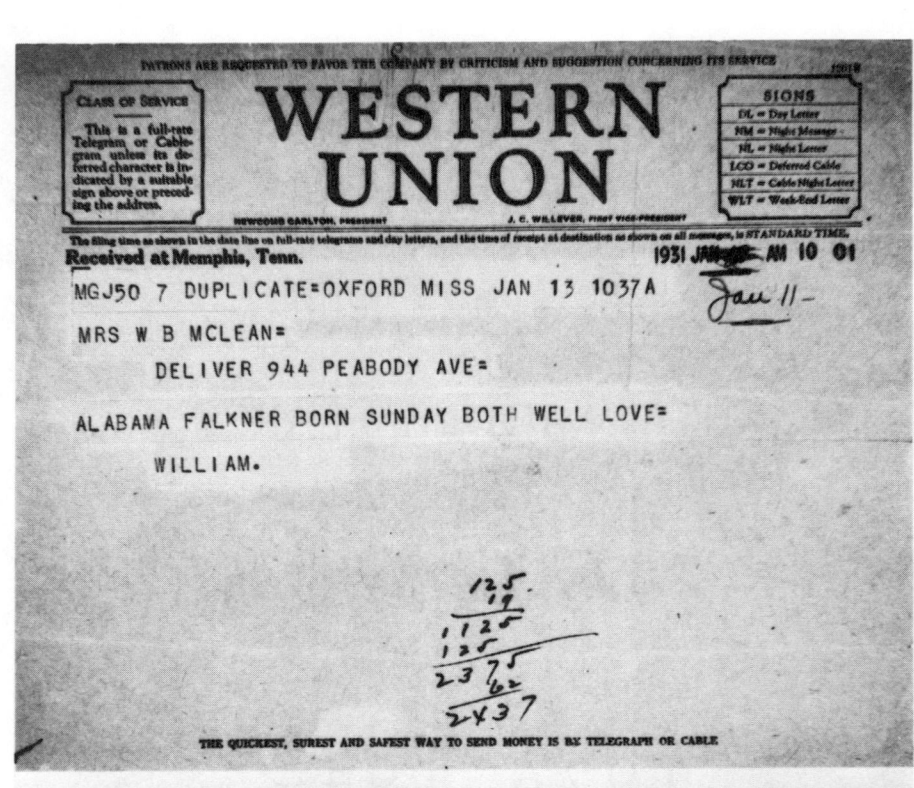
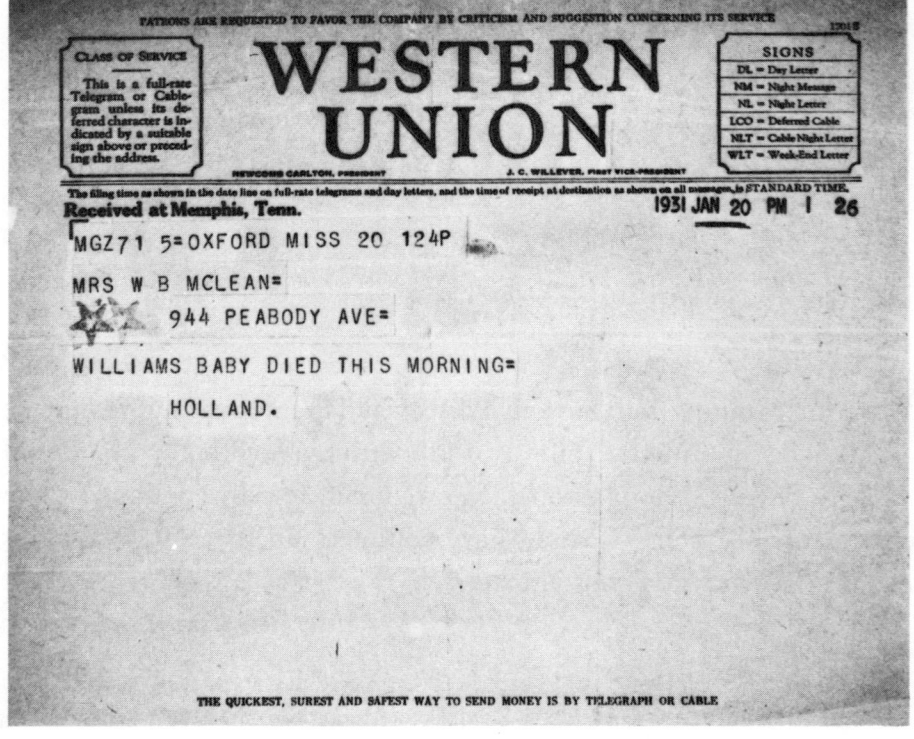

20 Telegrams announcing birth and death of Faulkner's first child

III

THE MIDDLE YEARS: *Fictionist*

William Faulkner's first novel, *Soldiers' Pay*, a story of postwar disillusionment, was published in 1926. His second novel, *Mosquitoes*, a satire upon would-be artists and dilettantes living in New Orleans, appeared the following year. Both works evidenced talent, but neither gave promise of the great achievements to come. Then in 1929, having been advised by Sherwood Anderson to concentrate on "that little patch up there in Mississippi where you started from," Faulkner produced *Sartoris*, the first of an extended series of novels and stories set in the fictional north Mississippi county of Yoknapatawpha.

During the next dozen years, in a flood of creative energy perhaps unrivaled in the history of American letters, Faulkner produced the major works on which his critical reputation is primarily based. In *The Sound and the Fury* (1929), generally recognized as his greatest novel, Faulkner employed the stream-of-consciousness technique utilized by James Joyce and T. S. Eliot to narrate the tragic decline of the once-aristocratic Compson family. In *As I Lay Dying* (1930), the tragicomic account of the Bundrens' epic journey to bury a family member, Faulkner added new variations to the stream-of-consciousness mode. Other Yoknapatawpha titles followed, including *Sanctuary* (1931), a shocking allegory treating the fate of innocence in a fallen world; *Light in August* (1932), a moving exposé of racial hatred and injustice; *Absalom, Absalom!* (1936), the account of the rise and fall of a nineteenth century planter named Thomas Sutpen; *The Unvanquished* (1938), the early history of the Sartoris clan; *The Hamlet* (1940), the first of three novels tracing the career of the nefarious Flem Snopes; and *Go Down, Moses* (1942), another sympathetic treatment of the Southern black. This last novel includes one section entitled "The Bear," which is universally acclaimed as one of the greatest short narratives in the English language.

On occasion during this period Faulkner stepped beyond the boundaries of his mythical Yoknapatawpha, as with the publication of *Pylon* (1935), a story of barnstorming pilots, and *The Wild Palms* (1939), significant for its experimental attempt to counterpoint and interlink two widely disparate narratives. Faulkner's middle years also saw the publication of a second volume of poems, *A Green Bough* (1933), and brief interludes of scriptwriting in Hollywood; but Faulkner never left Yoknapatawpha for long. Having discovered in his "little postage stamp of native soil" a microcosm of universal human behavior and meaning, he seldom needed to travel elsewhere.

1926

32 *Soldiers' Pay*.

New York: Boni & Liveright, [February 25] 1926.
First edition, first printing, with dust jacket.

> Inscribed copy given to Kenneth Godfrey. On title page, in black ink:
>
> > *William Faulkner*
> > *New York*
> > *7 Nov. 1931*

33 *Soldiers' Pay*.

New York: Boni & Liveright, 1926.
First edition, first printing, lacking dust jacket.

> Presentation copy. On title page, in blue ink:
>
> > *William Faulkner*
> > *Los Angeles Cal*
> > *26 May, 1932*
> >
> > *For Herb Starr*

34 *Soldiers' Pay*.

New York: Boni & Liveright, 1926.
First edition, second printing (April 1926), lacking dust jacket.

> Inscribed copy given to Myrtle Ramey. On title page, in blue ink:
>
> > *William Faulkner*

35 *Soldiers' Pay*.

New York: Horace Liveright, 1926.
First edition, third printing (April 1931), lacking dust jacket.

36 *Soldiers' Pay*.

London: Chatto and Windus, 1930.
Preface by Richard Hughes.
First British edition, first printing, with dust jacket.

> Inscribed by Hughes on free front endpaper, in black ink: "Pumpkin, with love. / D / June 1930."

37 *Monnaie de singe*.

Grenoble-Paris: Arthaud, 1948.
Trans. with introduction by Maxime Gaucher.

Fictionist, 1926–1944

First French edition, with blue band indicating "Un nouveau Faulkner vient de paraître."

Number 247 of limited issue of 300 copies on "vélin à la forme B. K. F. des Papeteries de Rives."

38 *Sherwood Anderson & Other Famous Creoles: A Gallery of Contemporary New Orleans.*

New Orleans: The Pelican Bookshop Press, [December 16] 1926.
Drawings by William Spratling; arrangement and foreword by Faulkner.
First edition, first issue.

Decorative rose boards with silver designs. Cover title printed in black on green paper label. Number 25 of first issue of 250 copies. Frontispiece and sixteen of the illustrations are hand-tinted by Spratling.
Presentation copy. On front flyleaf, in Spratling's hand, in blue ink: "W. P Spratling." On dedication page, in brown ink: "and including / Josiah Titzell / for whom / this copy / is affectionately / inscribed / by his friend / Bill Sprat / [rule]."
Laid in is hand-made Christmas card, featuring Spratling's drawing of a view of St. Peter's Street, and inscribed in Spratling's hand: "With love to you / & Lyle—"

39 *Sherwood Anderson & Other Famous Creoles: A Gallery of Contemporary New Orleans.*

New Orleans: The Pelican Bookshop Press, 1926.
Drawings by William Spratling; arrangement and foreword by Faulkner.
First edition, first issue.

Green boards with red label printed in black. Unnumbered out-of-series copy.
Inscribed on dedication page, in Spratling's hand, in blue ink: "and to my friend / [indecipherable], for / whom this copy is / inscribed— / W. P. Spratling— / New Orleans—Jan. 1927."
Laid in are two copies of prospectus which states: "A limited edition of 250 copies, bound in boards and done on imported paper, the first fifty decorated by hand with water color and autographed, at $5.00, the others at $2.00." On versos Spratling has listed the names of persons caricatured in the book, using numbers which correlate with numbers beside the names opposite the foreword in this copy of the book.

40 *Sherwood Anderson & Other Famous Creoles: A Gallery of Contemporary New Orleans.*

New Orleans: The Pelican Bookshop Press, 1926.
Drawings by William Spratling; arrangement and foreword by Faulkner.
First edition, first issue.

Green boards with white paper label. Spine paper missing. Number 119 of first issue of 250 copies.

41 *Sherwood Anderson & Other Famous Creoles: A Gallery of Contemporary New Orleans.*

New Orleans: The Pelican Bookshop Press, 1926.
Drawings by William Spratling; arrangement and foreword by Faulkner.
First edition, first issue.

>Green boards with red paper label. Number 138 of first issue of 250 copies.

42 *Sherwood Anderson & Other Famous Creoles: A Gallery of Contemporary New Orleans.*

New Orleans: The Pelican Bookshop Press, 1926.
Drawings by William Spratling; arrangement and foreword by Faulkner.
First edition, second issue.

>Green boards with white paper label. Paste-over label on certificate of limitation page states: "SECOND ISSUE 150 COPIES / JANUARY 1927."

1 9 2 7

43 *Mosquitoes.*

New York: Boni and Liveright, [April 30] 1927.
First edition, first printing, lacking dust jacket.

>Presentation copy given to 'Bama McLean, ca. 1927. On half title page, in blue ink:
>
>>*To Aunt Bama, with much love*
>>*Bill Faulkner*

44 *Mosquitoes.*

New York: Boni and Liveright, 1927.
First edition, first printing, lacking dust jacket.

>Presentation copy. On half title page, in blue ink:
>
>>*To Herb Starr,*
>>*from his friend, Bill Faulkner*
>
>On title page, in blue ink:
>
>>*William Faulkner*
>>*Sta. Monica, Cal.*
>>*23 July, 1934*

45 *Mosquitoes.*

New York: Boni and Liveright, 1927.
First edition, first printing, with original dust jacket (mosquito design).

46 *Mosquitoes.*

New York: Boni and Liveright, 1927.

First edition, first printing, with alternate dust jacket (cartoon showing four bridge players aboard a yacht) from later printing by Horace Liveright, Inc.

47 *Mosquitoes.*

London: Chatto & Windus, 1964.
Introduction by Richard Hughes.
First British edition, first printing, with dust jacket.

48 *Moustiques.*

Paris: Éditions de Minuit, 1948.
Trans. Jean Dubramet. Introduction by Raymond Queneau.
First French edition, with original glassine.

Number 26 of limited issue of 50 copies on "vélin supérieur de Corée."

49 *Moustiques.*

Paris: Éditions de Minuit, 1948.
Trans. Jean Dubramet. Introduction by Raymond Queneau.
First French edition, with original glassine.

Number 126 of limited issue of 150 copies on "Alfa-mousse des Papeteries de Navarre."

1 9 2 9

50 *Sartoris.*

New York: Harcourt, Brace and Company, [January 31] 1929.
First edition, first printing, lacking dust jacket.

Presentation copy given to Edith Brown. On free front endpaper, in blue ink:

> *To my good friend, Edith.*
> *from Bill*

On title page, in blue ink:

> *William Faulkner*
> *28 May 1929*

Also on free front endpaper, in Miss Brown's hand, in black ink: "Edith M. Brown / 1929."

51 *Sartoris.*

New York: Harcourt, Brace and Company, 1929.
First edition, first printing, with dust jacket.

Inscribed copy. On title page, in black ink:

>*William Faulkner*
>*30 July 1929*

52 *Sartoris.*

New York: Harcourt, Brace and Company, 1929.
First edition, first printing, lacking dust jacket.

Inscribed copy given to Myrtle Ramey Demarest. On title page, in blue ink:

>*William Faulkner*
>*Oxford, Miss*
>*17 May 1931*

On front paste-down, in Mrs. Demarest's hand, printed in black ink: "Myrtle Ramey Demarest."

53 *Sartoris.*

New York: Harcourt, Brace and Company, 1929.
First edition, first printing, lacking dust jacket.

Presentation copy. On title page, in blue ink:

>*William Faulkner*
>*Los Angeles, Cal*
>*May 26, 1932*
>
>*For Herb Starr*

54 *Sartoris.*

New York: Harcourt, Brace and Company, 1929.
First edition, first printing, with dust jacket.

55 *Sartoris.*

New York: Grosset & Dunlap, [ca. 1933].
First edition, reprint, lacking dust jacket.

Top edge stained purple.

56 *Sartoris.*

New York: Grosset & Dunlap, [ca. 1933].
First edition, reprint, lacking dust jacket.

Top edge stained violet.

57 *Sartoris.*

New York: Harcourt, Brace and Company, 1951.
First edition, reprint, with dust jacket.

Front of jacket displays quotation from Malcolm Cowley.

Fictionist, 1926–1944

58 *Sartoris*.

London: Chatto & Windus, 1932.
First edition, first British reprint, with dust jacket.

Blue cloth. Gold lettering stamped on spine. Top edge stained dark blue. Two leaves of advertisements inserted after p. 380.

59 *Sartoris*.

London: Chatto & Windus, 1932.
First edition, first British reprint, with dust jacket.

Cheap edition. Tan cloth. Red lettering stamped on spine. Edges unstained. Without advertisements.

60 *Sartoris*.

Paris: Gallimard, 1937.
Trans. R. N. Raimbault and H. Delgove.
First French edition, lacking glassine.

S. P. copy.
Presentation copy. On free front endpaper, in brown ink:

> *To Malcolm Franklin*
> *William Faulkner*
> *Oxford, Miss*
> *20 March 1946*

Also on free front endpaper, in Franklin's hand, in brown ink: "M. A. Franklin / Box 124 / Oxford, Miss."

61 *Sartoris*.

Paris: Gallimard, 1937.
Trans. R. N. Raimbault and H. Delgove.
First French edition, with original glassine.

S. P. copy, with publication notice laid in.
Inscribed by both translators. On half title page, in brown ink: "a [indecipherable] Yves Lawson / [indecipherable] hommage / des traducteurs / R. N. Raimbault." Below this inscription, in blue ink: "Henri Delgove."

62 *The Sound and the Fury*.

New York: Jonathan Cape and Harrison Smith, [October 7] 1929.
First edition, first printing, lacking dust jacket.

Presentation copy given to Calvin Brown. On front flyleaf, in blue ink:

> *To Dr Brown,*
> *sincerely,*
> *William Faulkner*
> *30 Oct 1929*

On title page, in blue ink:

> William Faulkner
> 30 Oct 1929

On half title page, in another hand, in pencil: "Brown."

63 *The Sound and the Fury.*

New York: Jonathan Cape and Harrison Smith, 1929.
First edition, first printing, lacking dust jacket.

Presentation copy. On title page, in blue ink:

> William Faulkner
> Los Angeles
> 26 May 1932
>
> *For Herb Starr*

On front flyleaf, in Starr's hand, in blue ink: "Hubert Starr / Oct 4–1929. / Los Angeles."

64 *The Sound and the Fury.*

New York: Jonathan Cape and Harrison Smith, 1929.
First edition, first printing, lacking dust jacket.

Copy belonged to 'Bama McLean. Inscribed on half title page, in Mrs. McLean's hand, in black ink: "Bama F. McLean / [rule]."

65 *The Sound and the Fury.*

New York: Jonathan Cape and Harrison Smith, 1929.
First edition, first printing, with dust jacket.

66 *The Sound and the Fury.*

New York: Jonathan Cape and Harrison Smith, 1929.
First edition, third printing (November 1931), lacking dust jacket.

Presentation copy. On half title page, in blue ink (see plate 31):

> *To Malcolm Cowley*
> *Who beat me to what*
> *was to have been the*
> *leisurely pleasure of my*
> *old age.*
>
> William Faulkner

On title page, in blue ink:

> William Faulkner
> Oxford, Miss
> 16 March 1946

Fictionist, 1926–1944

On front flyleaf and on half title page, in Cowley's hand, in pencil: "Malcolm Cowley."

Faulkner's inscription relates to Cowley's production of *The Portable Faulkner*. The story of this copy of *The Sound and the Fury* and its inscription is recounted in *The Faulkner-Cowley File*, pp. 86–87, 90–91.

67 *The Sound and the Fury.*

London: Chatto and Windus, 1931.
Introduction by Richard Hughes.
First British edition, first printing, with dust jacket.

68 *Le bruit et la fureur.*

Paris: Gallimard, 1938.
Trans. with preface by Maurice E. Coindreau.
First French edition, with original glassine.

S.P. copy, with publication notice laid in.
Inscribed by translator on free front endpaper, in blue ink: "A / M. Yves Gandon / Hommage du traducteur / M E Coindreau / [rule]."

1930

69 Lease contract. Unsigned carbon typescript, 3 pages, 14 by 8½ inches, watermarked "Fidelity Onion Skin."

Between Faulkner and [Walter B.] Mayfield; for house and land on Oxford and Toccopola road, east of Oxford. Covers five-year period and includes option to purchase. Drawn for Faulkner by Phil Stone and dated "January___, 1930."

This transaction was never closed. On April 12, 1930, Faulkner signed the papers to secure Rowan Oak instead.

70 "A Rose for Emily."

Forum, 83 (April 1930), 233–238.

First publication of story collected in *These 13*.

71 "Honor."

American Mercury, 20 (July 1930), 268–274.

First publication of story collected in *Doctor Martino and Other Stories*.

72 *As I Lay Dying.*

New York: Jonathan Cape and Harrison Smith, [October 6] 1930.
First edition, first printing, lacking dust jacket.

First state of printing, with large capital "I" on page 11 dropped from correct alignment.

Presentation copy given to Phil Stone. Edges badly burned in the fire which destroyed the Stone house in 1942. On free front endpaper, in blue ink:

To Phil, with love
from Bill

On title page, in blue ink:

William Faulkner
10 October, 1930

73 *As I Lay Dying.*

New York: Jonathan Cape and Harrison Smith, 1930.
First edition, first printing, with dust jacket.

First state of printing. Top edge stained dark brown. Also, on the cover of this copy the word "I" has top serif missing.
Inscribed copy given to Myrtle Ramey Demarest. On title page, in blue ink:

William Faulkner
Oxford, Miss
17 May, 1931

74 *As I Lay Dying.*

New York: Jonathan Cape and Harrison Smith, 1930.
First edition, first printing, lacking dust jacket.

First state of printing.
Presentation copy. On front paste-down, in blue ink:

To Herb, from Bill Faulkner

On title page, in blue ink:

William Faulkner
Los Angeles,   May, 1932

Also on front paste-down, in Starr's hand, in black ink: "Hubert Starr / Los Angeles / September, 1930."

75 *As I Lay Dying.*

New York: Jonathan Cape and Harrison Smith, 1930.
First edition, first printing, with dust jacket.

First state of printing.

76 *As I Lay Dying.*

New York: Jonathan Cape and Harrison Smith, 1930.
First edition, first printing, with dust jacket.

First state of printing. Top serif missing from word "I" on cover.

Fictionist, 1926–1944

77 *As I Lay Dying.*

New York: Jonathan Cape and Harrison Smith, 1930.
First edition, first printing, with dust jacket.

    Second state of printing, with "I" on page 11 properly aligned. Top edge stained dark brown.
    Inscribed copy given to Myrtle Ramey Demarest. On title page, in blue ink:

> *William Faulkner*
> *13 November 1930*

78 *As I Lay Dying.*

New York: Jonathan Cape and Harrison Smith, 1930.
First edition, first printing, lacking dust jacket.

    Second state of printing. Top edge stained light brown.
    Presentation copy. On free front endpaper, in blue ink:

> *To Jim Devine,*
> *Baron of Hoboken,*
> *from his friend Bill Faulkner,*
> *Earl of Beerinstein*

    The story of this inscription is recounted in Blotner, *Faulkner: A Biography*, pp. 738–739.

79 *As I Lay Dying.*

New York: Jonathan Cape and Harrison Smith, 1930.
First edition, first printing, with dust jacket.

    Second state of printing. Top edge stained light brown.

80 *As I Lay Dying.*

New York: Harrison Smith & Robert Haas, 1930.
First edition, second printing (January 1933), lacking dust jacket.

81 *As I Lay Dying.*

London: Chatto & Windus, 1935.
First British edition, first printing, lacking dust jacket.

    Presentation copy. On free front endpaper, in black ink:

> *For my son, Malcolm Franklin*
> *William Faulkner*
> *Oxford, Miss*
> *20 March 1946*

    On title page, in blue ink:

> *William Faulkner*

Also on free front endpaper, in Franklin's hand, in black ink: "Malcolm A. Franklin / Rowan Oak / Oxford, Miss. / [rule] / 29 X State St. / Charleston, S. C."

82 *As I Lay Dying*.

London: Chatto & Windus, 1935.
First British edition, first printing, with dust jacket.

83 *Tandis que j'agonise*.

Paris: Gallimard, 1934.
Trans. Maurice E. Coindreau. Preface by Valery Larbaud.
First French edition, with original glassine.

S.P. copy, with "Hommage du Traducteur" card laid in.
Unnumbered copy of limited issue of 60 copies "hors commerce" on "alfa Lafuma-Navarre."
This was the first Faulkner title to be translated into French, but publication followed *Sanctuaire* in 1933.

84 *Tandis que j'agonise*.

Paris: Jean Boisseau, 1946.
Trans. M. E. Coindreau. Engravings by Pierre Courtin.
Unsewn gatherings, boxed.

Number 25 of limited issue of 25 copies on "auvergne à la main avec suite de toutes les gravures."
The engravings by Courtin, a noted French artist, make this volume one of the most attractive Faulkner books ever produced.

85 *Tandis que j'agonise*.

Paris: Jean Boisseau, 1946.
Trans. M. E. Coindreau. Engravings by Pierre Courtin.
Unsewn gatherings, in wrappers, with original glassine.

Number 42 of limited issue of 175 copies on "pur fil de lana."

1931

86 "Dry September."

Scribner's Magazine, 89 (January 1931), 49–56.

First publication of story collected in *These 13*.

87 Western Union Telegram from Faulkner to Mrs. Walter B. McLean (Aunt 'Bama), dated January 13, 1931.

Announces the birth of Faulkner's first child, Alabama.

Someone—perhaps Mrs. McLean—has crossed out the typed receipt line date "Jan. 19" [sic] and inked in beneath it "Jan 11." See plate 20.

88 Western Union Telegram from Holland [Wilkins], Faulkner's aunt, to Mrs. Walter B. McLean (Aunt 'Bama), dated January 20, 1931.

Announces the death of Faulkner's infant daughter, Alabama. See plate 20.

89 *Sanctuary*.

New York: Jonathan Cape & Harrison Smith, [February 9] 1931.
First edition, first printing, lacking dust jacket.

Presentation copy which belonged to Hubert Starr. On half title page, in blue ink:

To Herb, from Bill Faulkner

On title page, in blue ink:

William Faulkner
Sta. Monica, Cal.
23 July, 1934

90 *Sanctuary*.

New York: Jonathan Cape & Harrison Smith, 1931.
First edition, first printing, with dust jacket.

91 *Sanctuary*.

New York: Jonathan Cape & Harrison Smith, 1931.
First edition, second printing (February 1931), lacking dust jacket.

92 *Sanctuary*.

New York: Jonathan Cape & Harrison Smith, 1931.
First edition, third printing (February 1931), lacking dust jacket.

93 *Sanctuary*.

New York: Jonathan Cape & Harrison Smith, 1931.
First edition, fourth printing (March 1931), with dust jacket.

Inscribed copy given to Myrtle Ramey Demarest. On title page, in blue ink:

William Faulkner
Oxford, Miss
10 April 1931

94 *Sanctuary*.

New York: Jonathan Cape & Harrison Smith, 1931.

First edition, fourth printing, lacking dust jacket.

Presentation copy given to 'Bama McLean. On title page, in blue ink:

> *Aunt Bama*
> *with love*
>
> William Faulkner
> Oxford, Miss
> 28 Nov 1947

95 *Sanctuary*.

New York: Jonathan Cape & Harrison Smith, 1931.
First edition, fifth printing (April 1931), lacking dust jacket.

96 *Sanctuary*.

New York: Jonathan Cape & Harrison Smith, 1931.
First edition, sixth printing (July 1931), with dust jacket.

97 *Sanctuary*.

New York: Grosset & Dunlap, [ca. 1946].
First edition, reprint, lacking dust jacket.

Reddish brown cloth. Top edge stained light brown.
Faulkner gave this copy to Phil Stone to replace the original edition which was destroyed when Stone's house burned in 1942. Contains Emily Stone's penciled notations.

98 *Sanctuary*.

New York: Grosset & Dunlap, [ca. 1946].
First edition, reprint, with dust jacket.

Reddish brown cloth. Top edge stained light brown.

99 *Sanctuary*.

New York: Grosset & Dunlap, [ca. 1946].
First edition, reprint, lacking dust jacket.

Variant binding. Tan cloth. Top edge stained light brown. This copy, printed on heavier paper, is noticeably larger than the Grosset & Dunlap copies listed above.

100 *Sanctuary*.

London: Chatto and Windus, 1931.
First British edition, first printing, lacking dust jacket.

Bowdlerized text.
Two leaves of advertisements tipped in after p. 316.

Fictionist, 1926–1944

101 *Sanctuary*.

Paris: Crosby Continental Editions, 1932.
First edition, only printing, in printed wrappers.

   English text.

102 *Sanctuaire*.

Paris: Gallimard, 1933.
Trans. R. N. Raimbault and Henri Delgove. Preface by André Malraux.
First French edition, with original glassine.

   Unnumbered S.P. copy.
   Inscribed by both translators. On front flyleaf: "a Norman Pierre Loiseles / avec les hommage de / R N Raimbault / Henri Delgove / [rule]."

103 *Sanctuaire*.

Paris: Gallimard, 1933.
Trans. R. N. Raimbault and Henri Delgove. Preface by André Malraux.
First French edition, lacking original glassine.

   S.P. copy.
   Unnumbered copy of limited issue of 67 copies "hors commerce" on "alfa Navarre."

104 "That Evening Sun Go Down."

American Mercury, 22 (March 1931), 257–267.

   First publication of story collected, in somewhat altered form, in *These 13*.

105 "Ad Astra."

American Caravan IV, ed. Alfred Kreymborg, Lewis Mumford, and Paul Rosenfeld. New York: The Macaulay Company, 1931, pp. 164–181. First edition, first printing.

   Number 80 of limited edition of 250 signed copies. This copy signed by Rosenfeld and Mumford. Typed note laid in explains that Kreymborg was in Europe and unavailable to autograph this copy.
   First publication of story collected in *These 13*.

106 "Hair."

American Mercury, 23 (May 1931), 53–61.

   First publication of story collected in *These 13*.

107 "Spotted Horses."

Scribner's Magazine, 89 (June 1931), 585–597.

June 17, 1931

Mr. E. Byrne Hackett
℅ Brick Row Book Shop, Inc.
30 Broadway,
New York, New York

Dear Mr. Hackett:

You doubtless remember that when William Faulkner first conceived the idea that he wanted to write I was the one who lent him books, and encouraged him. I read all of his stuff, advised and criticized furnished him with money off and on and generally carried him forward until he was self-sustaining both financially and artistically.

He started out with the idea that he wanted to be a poet — according to the proverb that all good novelists are poets in their youth. The first book he had published was a little group of poems, "The Marble Faun". In 1924. I put up the money to pay the Four Seas Company for publishing one thousand copies and this was the only edition published.

At the time I tried to sell as many copies as possible in order to get my money back. Especially I tried to interest the friends of myself and Bill in the book and Bill autographed several presentation copies most of which we sold. Some of the people did not pay for their copies and I have on hand four autographed presentation copies besides my own. We have had several financial reverses and I am willing to sell these four copies — I would not sell my own copy, of course — if the price offered justifies.

Even at a high price these copies would be a good buy for a collector. Bill is already one of the leading figures in American literature. He is already established and his reputation is going to grow because the achievement will be forthcoming.

In addition to that he was always very stingy with autographs and has quit altogether now. He says that he is not going to give any more autographs except to me, his mother and four or five friends. So the autographs will grow rarer and rarer and if any collector want autographs from him they had better get them now.

Also this is the only book of verse he has had published and it is probable that it will always be the only one. He has written no verse for years and will probably never write any more.

Bill told me that a copy of "The Marble Faun" unautographed, sold not long ago for twenty-five dollars.

Page 2.

I am going to sell these four copies to somebody but Bill and I both remember you most pleasantly and he wanted me to give you the first chance at them. If you want them make me a price.

Also, if you wish, I will also autograph each of them since I wrote the preface and will authorize you to sell this letter with the books. This is only for you as a matter of friendship for you on the part of Bill and myself and to give you the chance to make some money and I will not do this for anyone but you or Al Delaney to whom I shall offer the books next if you are not interested.

Bill and I think of you frequently and hope that you are doing well. Whenever we come to New York again we shall come to see you.

Your friend,

PS:WS

21 Letter from Phil Stone to E. Byrne Hackett concerning *The Marble Faun*

First publication of story which became a part of *The Hamlet*.

108 Letters from Phil Stone concerning *The Marble Faun*.

a. To E. Byrne Hackett, July 17, 1931, unsigned carbon typescript, 2 pages (see plate 21).

b. To Paul Leahy, July 29, 1931, unsigned carbon typescript, 2 pages.

c. To Henry Malcheski, August 5, 1931, unsigned carbon typescript, 2 pages.

d. To G. C. Buzby, August 27, 1931, unsigned carbon typescript, 2 pages.

In these letters Stone summarizes the history of the publication of Faulkner's first book and offers to sell the copies in his possession for $75.00 each.

109 "The Hound."

Harper's Magazine, 163 (August 1931), 266–274.

First publication of story collected in *Doctor Martino and Other Stories*. Rewritten and incorporated into *The Hamlet*.

110 "Fox Hunt."

Harper's Magazine, 163 (September 1931), 392–402.

First publication of story collected in *Doctor Martino and Other Stories*.

111 *These 13*.

New York: Jonathan Cape & Harrison Smith, [September 21] 1931.
First edition, presumably first printing. The limited and trade copies of this book were printed separately.

Number 99 of signed, limited issue of 299 copies.
First publication of "Victory," "All the Dead Pilots," "Crevasse," "A Justice," "Mistral," "Divorce in Naples," and "Carcassonne." The other stories—"Ad Astra," "Red Leaves," "A Rose for Emily," "Hair," "That Evening Sun," and "Dry September"—were previously published.

112 *These 13*.

New York: Jonathan Cape & Harrison Smith, 1931.
First edition, first trade printing, lacking dust jacket.

Dedication page reads: "To Estelle and Alabama." (Alabama was Faulkner's first child, who was born prematurely and lived only nine days. She was named after Faulkner's beloved great-aunt, 'Bama McLean. See items 87 and 88.)
Presentation copy. On half title page, in blue ink:

To Aunt Bama,
with love.
William

On title page, in blue ink:

> *William Faulkner*
> *Oxford, Miss*
> *September 29, 1931*

113 *These 13.*

New York: Jonathan Cape & Harrison Smith, 1931.
First edition, first trade printing, with dust jacket.

114 *These 13.*

New York: Jonathan Cape & Harrison Smith, 1931.
First edition, "Second Printing, September, 1931," lacking dust jacket.

Resembles first printing, trade edition, in all respects, including blue figured design on gray endpapers.

115 *These 13.*

New York: Jonathan Cape & Harrison Smith, 1931.
First edition, "Third Printing, October, 1931," lacking dust jacket.

Blue cloth with white cloth spine. Orange lettering. Top edge stained dark blue. Blue figured design on gray endpapers.
Presentation copy. On title page, in black ink:

> *To Jim Devine*
> *from his friend*
> *Bill Faulkner*
> *New York*
> *7 Nov 1937*

116 *These 13.*

New York: Jonathan Cape & Harrison Smith, 1931.
First edition, "Third Printing, October, 1931," lacking dust jacket.

Variant binding. Black cloth with gold lettering. Edges unstained. Gray endpapers with blue figured design, as in first printing, trade edition.

117 *Treize histoires.*

Paris: Gallimard, 1939.
Trans. R.-N. Raimbault, Ch.-P. Vorce, and M.-E. Coindreau. Preface by Raimbault.
First French edition, with original glassine.

Unnumbered S.P. copy.

118 *Treize histoires.*

Paris: Gallimard, 1939.

Trans. R.-N. Raimbault, Ch.-P. Vorce, and M.-E. Coindreau. Preface by Raimbault.
First French edition, with original glassine.

Number 53 of limited issue of 20 copies (numbered 51–70) "hors commerce" on "alfa des Papeteries Lafuma Navarre."
Inscribed on half title page, in black ink: "A [indecipherable] L. D. Hirsch / Le cordial hommage de / R N. Raimbault."

119 "Doctor Martino."

Harper's Magazine, 163 (November 1931), 733–743.

First publication of story collected in *Doctor Martino and Other Stories*.

120 Letter from Phil Stone to Faulkner, dated November 2, 1931, unsigned carbon typescript, 1 page.

Solicits names of potential buyers of *The Marble Faun* and expresses interest in doing reviews and literary "hack work."

121 *Idyll in the Desert*.

New York: Random House, [December 10] 1931.
Only edition, only printing, lacking glassine.

Number 305 of signed, limited edition of 400 copies.
First Faulkner title under Random House imprint. Next one: *Absalom, Absalom!*, 1936.

1 9 3 2

122 "Death Drag."

Scribner's Magazine, 91 (January 1932), 34–42.

First publication of story collected in *Doctor Martino and Other Stories*.

123 *Contempo*, 1 (February 1, 1932).

First publication of nine poems and one story by Faulkner.

Poems:

   a. "I Will Not Weep for Youth," 1. Reprinted in *An Anthology of the Younger Poets* and *Lillabulero*.

   b. "Knew I Love Once," 1. Reprinted in *An Anthology of the Younger Poets*. Became XXXIII, *A Green Bough*.

   c. "Twilight," 1. Reprinted in *An Anthology of the Younger Poets*. Became X, *A Green Bough*.

d. "Visions in Spring," 1. Reprinted in *Lillabulero*.

e. "To A Virgin," 2. Reprinted in *An Anthology of the Younger Poets*. Became XXXIX, *A Green Bough*.

f. "Winter is Gone," 2. Reprinted in *An Anthology of the Younger Poets* and *Lillabulero*.

g. "My Epitaph," 2. Reprinted in *An Anthology of the Younger Poets*. Considerably revised when published as *This Earth*. Became XLIV, *A Green Bough*. This last version appears as "If There Be Grief" in *Mississippi Verse*.

h. "Spring," 2. Became XXXVI, *A Green Bough*.

i. "April," 2. Reprinted in *Lillabulero*.

Story: "Once Aboard the Lugger," 1f. Reprinted in *Lillabulero*.

124 Wells, Oliver, ed. *An Anthology of the Younger Poets*. Philadelphia: The Centaur Press, 1932. Preface by Archibald MacLeish. First edition, with glassine.

> Number 259 of limited edition of 500 copies.
> Includes, on pages 122–126, six of the nine Faulkner poems printed in the February 1, 1932, issue of *Contempo* (see item **123**).

125 Wells, Oliver, ed. *An Anthology of the Younger Poets*. Philadelphia: The Centaur Press, 1932. Preface by Archibald MacLeish. First edition, with glassine.

> Back flyleaf of this copy contains no printed certificate of limitation.

126 "Centaur in Brass."

American Mercury, 25 (February 1932), 200–210.

> First publication of story later reworked and incorporated into *The Town*.

127 "Lizards in Jamshyd's Courtyard."

The Saturday Evening Post, 204 (February 27, 1932), 12ff.

> First publication of story revised and incorporated into *The Hamlet*.

128 "A Rose for Emily."

The Golden Book Magazine, 15 (March 1932), 223–228.

> One of the earliest reprints of this popular story.

129 "Smoke."

Harper's Magazine, 164 (April 1932), 562–578.

First publication of story collected in *Doctor Martino and Other Stories*. Also included in *Knight's Gambit*.

130 *Salmagundi*.

Milwaukee: The Casanova Press, [April 30] 1932.
Only edition, only printing, with maroon slip case.

Number 25 of limited edition of 525 copies. One of the first 26 copies, in which top edges of pages are even with wrappers and trimmed, while bottoms of pages are uneven and untrimmed.
Reprints five poems and three prose pieces by Faulkner. Poetry: "The Faun," "Portrait," "Dying Gladiator," "The Lilacs," and "L'Apres-Midi d'un Faune." Prose: "New Orleans," "On Criticism," and "Verse Old and Nascent: A Pilgrimage."

131 *Salmagundi*.

Milwaukee: The Casanova Press, 1932.
Only edition, only printing, with maroon slip case.

Number 30 of limited edition of 525 copies.
Presentation copy. On cover, in blue ink (see plate 22):

> *To Hubert Starr, from William Faulkner*
> *Sta. Monica,*
> *23 July, 1934*

132 "A Child Looks from His Window."

Contempo, 2 (May 25, 1932), 3.

First publication of this poem. Reprinted in *Lillabulero*.

133 *Miss Zilphia Gant*.

Dallas: The Book Club of Texas, [June 27] 1932.
Preface by Henry Nash Smith.
Only edition in English, only printing, with original glassine.

Number 60 of limited edition of 300 copies.
Accompanied by prospectus showing a specimen page and announcing delivery date as June 15, 1932, and by broadside listing information about the Book Club of Texas and soliciting members.

134 *Light in August*.

New York: Harrison Smith & Robert Haas, [October 6] 1932.
First edition, first printing, with dust jacket and original glassine.

Presentation copy given to Phil Stone. On free front endpaper, in blue-black ink:

> *To Phil, from Bill*
> *12 Dec. 1932*

22 Cover of *Salmagundi*. Inscribed by Faulkner to Hubert Starr.

On title page, in blue-black ink:

> *William Faulkner*
> *Oxford, Miss*
> *12 Dec. 1932*

135 *Light in August.*

New York: Harrison Smith & Robert Haas, 1932.
First edition, first printing, with dust jacket and original glassine.

Presentation copy. On free front endpaper, in blue ink:

> *For Myrtle Ramey,*
> *Oxford, Miss.   30 March [?] 1934*
> *William Faulkner*

136 *Light in August.*

New York: Harrison Smith & Robert Haas, 1932.
First edition, first printing, with dust jacket and original glassine.

Presentation copy. On title page, in black ink:

> *For Malcolm Cowley*
> *William Faulkner*
> *Sherman, Conn*
> *25 Oct. 1948*

137 *Light in August.*

New York: Harrison Smith & Robert Haas, 1932.
First edition, first printing, with dust jacket.

138 *Light in August.*

New York: Harrison Smith & Robert Haas, 1932.
First edition, second printing (October 1932), lacking dust jacket.

Stamped on both front and spine in blue. Top edge stained orange.

139 *Light in August.*

New York: Harrison Smith & Robert Haas, 1932.
First edition, fourth printing (October 1932), lacking dust jacket.

Stamped on both front and spine in blue, as in second printing. Top edge stained orange.

140 *Light in August.*

New York: Harrison Smith & Robert Haas, 1932.
First edition, fourth printing (October 1932), lacking dust jacket.

Green cloth stamped in dark green on front and spine. Top edge unstained.

Title page lists publisher as Harrison Smith & Robert Haas, but spine shows Random House imprint. Obviously this copy was made from the unused sheets from the fourth printing but was not bound and distributed until sometime after Random House became Faulkner's publisher in 1936.

141   *Light in August*.

New York: The Modern Library, 1950.
Introduction by Richard H. Rovere.
First Modern Library edition (number 88), with dust jacket.

142   *Lumière d'août*.

Paris: Gallimard, 1935.
Trans. with introduction by Maurice E. Coindreau.
First French edition, lacking original glassine.

Number 41 of limited issue of 50 copies.

143   "A Mountain Victory."

The Saturday Evening Post, 205 (December 3, 1932), 6ff.

First publication of story collected in *Doctor Martino and Other Stories*.

144   *This Earth*.

New York: Equinox, [December] 1932.
Illustrated by Albert Heckman.

Pamphlet, 8 pages, in printed wrappers, with plain white envelope in which it was issued.

Slightly revised version of poem, "My Epitaph."

1 9 3 3

145   "There Was a Queen."

Scribner's Magazine, 93 (January 1933), 10–16.

First publication of story collected in *Doctor Martino and Other Stories*.

146   Portrait photograph of Faulkner, 7 by 5 inches. Given by Faulkner to 'Bama McLean. See plate 23.

Inscribed by Faulkner, in blue ink:

> *To Aunt Bama,*
> *from William Faulkner*
> *Oxford, Miss.   27 Jan. 1933*

23 Cofield photograph of Faulkner. Inscribed to 'Bama McLean, 1933.

Imprint stamped on verso: "Cofield's Studio / Oxford, Miss." Also typed on verso: "William Faulkner / Oxford, Miss." and "Please return this photo to / H. Wilson Roberts, / Oxford, Mississippi / WITHOUT FAIL, PLEASE!"

147 *A Green Bough*.

New York: Harrison Smith and Robert Haas, [April 20] 1933.
First edition, first printing, limited issue. The limited and trade copies of this book may be separate printings, but no priority has been established.

Unnumbered out-of-series copy of signed, limited issue of 360 copies.
A *Green Bough* contains forty-four poems, many of which Faulkner had written a decade or more earlier. Most of the poems were revised for publication in this volume. Fifteen of the poems had been previously published.
The Brodsky Collection includes early manuscripts of twelve poems which appear in *A Green Bough*. These are listed below according to the number assigned the poem in *A Green Bough* and the manuscript title or first line(s).

I	"We had been / Raiding over Mannheim" ["The Lilacs"]. See item **13**.
VIII	"He furrows the brown earth, doubly sweet." See item **21e**.
IX	"The sun lay long upon the hills." See item **11a**.
XI	"When evening shadows grew around." See item **11d**.
XIII	"When I was young and proud and gay." See item **11f**.
XIV	"The Gallows." See item **21h**.
XXVIII	"Wild Geese" ["Over the World's Rim"]. See item **21d**.
XXIX	"Pregna[n]cy." See item **21i**.
XXX	"November 11th" ["Gray the Day"].-See item **21j**.
XXXV	"Indian Summer." See item **21c**.
XLII	"March." See item **21l**.
XLIV	"Mississippi Hills: My Epitaph." See item **21g**.

148 *A Green Bough*.

New York: Harrison Smith and Robert Haas, 1933.
First edition, first trade printing, lacking dust jacket.

Presentation copy. On free front endpaper, in blue ink (see plate 24):

For Aunt Bama
with love

William

[slanted arrow pointed above]

not through mistake but affection,
besides she owns us both anyway.

To Cousin Vance Carter Broach
From Cousin William Faulkner

On title page, in blue ink:

William Faulkner
Oxford, Miss   28 Nov 1947

For Aunt 'Bama
with love
William

not through mistake but affection,
besides she owns us both anyway.

To Cousin Vance Carter Broach
From Cousin William Faulkner

24   Inscription in *A Green Bough*

149 *A Green Bough.*

New York: Harrison Smith and Robert Haas, 1933.
First edition, first trade printing, lacking dust jacket.

> Advance review copy, with slip laid in showing publication date as April 20.

150 *A Green Bough.*

New York: Harrison Smith and Robert Haas, 1933.
First edition, "Second Printing, April 1933," lacking dust jacket.

> Inscribed copy which belonged to Eric "Jim" Devine. On title page, in black ink:
>
> *William Faulkner*
> *New York*
> *9 October 1938*

151 *Le rameau vert.*

Paris: Gallimard, 1955.
Trans. R. N. Raimbault.
First French edition, with original glassine.

> Contains both French and English texts.
> Number 64 of limited issue of 86 copies on "velin pur fil Lafuma-Navarre."

152 "Man Comes, Man Goes."

New Republic, 74 (May 3, 1933), 338.

> Poem which appears as VI, *A Green Bough*.

153 "The Flowers That Died."

Contempo, 3 (June 25, 1933), 1.

> Only publication of this poem.

1934

154 "Elly."

Story, 4 (February 1934), 3–15.

> First publication of story collected in *Doctor Martino and Other Stories*.

155 "Wash."

Harper's Magazine, 168 (February 1934), 258–266.

> First publication of story collected in *Doctor Martino and Other Stories*. **Also incorporated, in revised form, into *Absalom, Absalom!***

Fictionist, 1926–1944

156 *The Oxford Magazine*, 1 (April 1, 1934).

Contains Phil Stone's article, "William Faulkner: The Man and His Work." Also includes essays and artwork by Emily Whitehurst and Ella Somerville and a sketch of Faulkner by Sykes Kennon.

Copy belonged to Phil Stone.

157 *The Oxford Magazine*, 1 (April 1, 1934).

Copy belonged to Myrtle Ramey Demarest.

158 *Doctor Martino and Other Stories*.

New York: Harrison Smith and Robert Haas, [April 16] 1934.
First edition, first printing, limited issue. The limited and trade copies of this book may be separate printings, but no priority has been established.

Number 223 of signed, limited issue of 360 copies.
Doctor Martino and Other Stories includes fourteen stories, only two of which— "Leg" and "Black Music"—had not been previously published. Those reprinted are "Doctor Martino," "Fox Hunt," "The Hound," "Death Drag," "There Was a Queen," "Smoke," "Turn About," "Beyond," "Wash," "Elly," "Mountain Victory," and "Honor."

159 *Doctor Martino and Other Stories*.

New York: Harrison Smith and Robert Haas, 1934.
First edition, first trade printing, with dust jacket.

Presentation copy. On free front endpaper, in blue ink:

> *To Hubert Starr,*
> *from his friend, Bill Faulkner*

On title page, in blue ink:

> *William Faulkner*
> *Sta Monica, Cal.*
> *23 July 1934*

Also on title page, in Starr's hand, in blue ink: "Bot 4/17/34 / H.S."

160 *Doctor Martino and Other Stories*.

New York: Harrison Smith and Robert Haas, 1934.
First edition, first trade printing, with dust jacket.

161 *Doctor Martino and Other Stories*.

London: Chatto & Windus, 1934.
First edition, first British reprint, with dust jacket.

162 *Le docteur Martino et autres histoires*.

Paris: Gallimard, 1948.
Trans. R.-N. Raimbault and Ch.-P. Vorce.
First French edition, with original glassine.

>Number CLXXXI of limited issue of 210 copies on "vélin pur fil Lafuma Navarre."

163 Last will and testament of William Faulkner, dated "June___, 1934." Unsigned carbon typescript, 3 pages, 14 by 8½ inches, watermarked "MYRIAD CHEMCO."

>Prepared for Faulkner by Phil Stone.
>This document is summarized in Blotner, *Faulkner: A Biography*, p. 850.

164 "Mule in the Yard."

Scribner's Magazine, 96 (August 1934), 65–70.

>First publication of story later revised and incorporated into *The Town*.

165 "Ambuscade."

The Saturday Evening Post, 207 (September 29, 1934), 12ff.

>First publication of story which became part of *The Unvanquished*.

166 James, Alice, ed. *Mississippi Verse*. Chapel Hill: University of North Carolina Press, 1934. First edition, first printing, with dust jacket.

Reprints, on pages 31–34, seven poems from *A Green Bough*: "Mirror of Youth" (XVI); "The Courtesan Is Dead" (XXXV); "Green Is the Water" (XIX); "If There Be Grief" (XLIV); "Here He Stands" (XX); "Boy and Eagle" (XVIII); and "Mother and Child" (XXXIV).

>This copy, which belonged to Calvin Brown, was used as an autograph book by the owner. Inscribed by Brown, in black ink, on free front endpaper: "Calvin S. Brown, / 1934."
>On verso of half title page, in a variety of colors of ink, are the signatures of sixteen of the forty-three contributors, including that of Faulkner (see plate 25).
>On back two flyleaves, one of which is tipped in, appear the signatures—dated from 1934 to 1939—of numerous "Friends of Culture," including Emily Whitehurst, Edith Brown, A. Wigfall Green, Cleanth Brooks, Roark Bradford, Caroline Tate, Allen Tate, John Gould Fletcher, Lyle Saxon, Robert Penn Warren, Herschel Brickell, and others.
>On title page and on page vii appears the signature of Alice James, the editor.

1 9 3 5

167 *Pylon*.

New York: Harrison Smith and Robert Haas, Inc., [March 25] 1935.
First edition, first printing, limited issue, boxed. The limited and trade copies of this book may be separate printings, but no priority has been established.

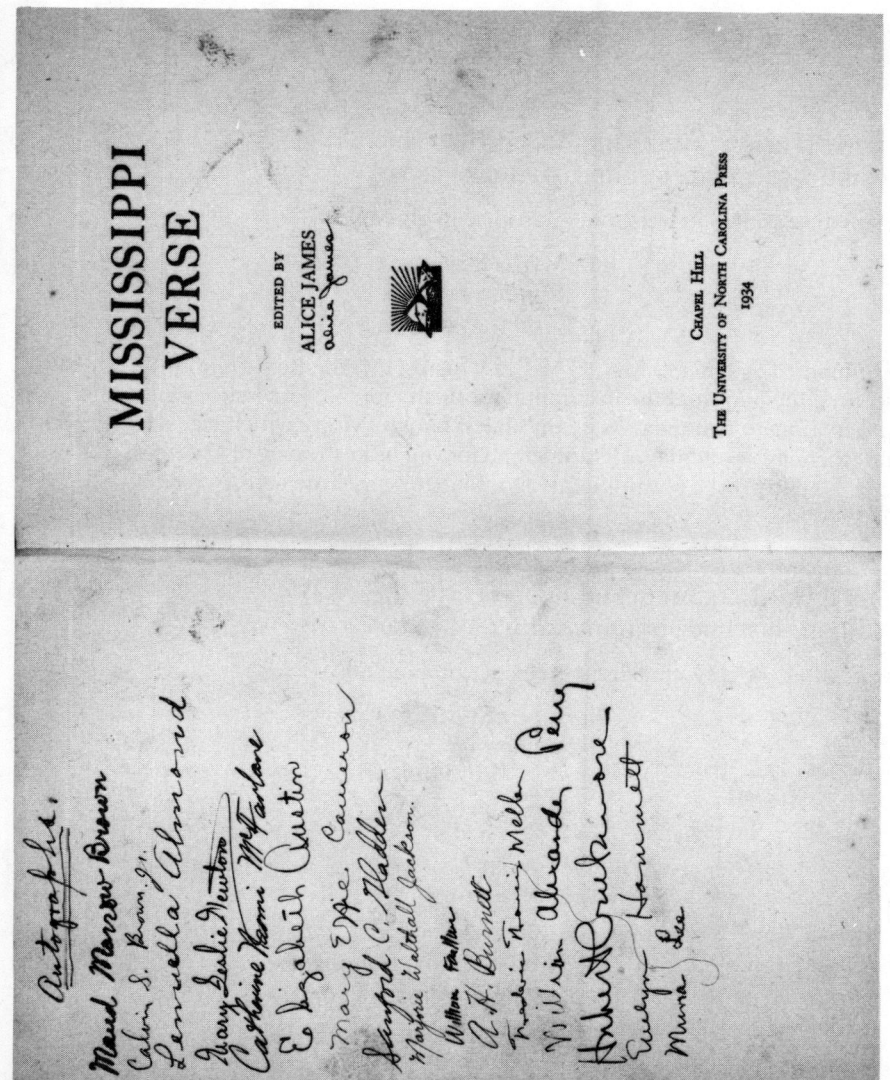

25 Title page of *Mississippi Verse*, with autographs of several contributors, including Faulkner

Number 294 of signed, limited issue of 310 copies.

168 *Pylon.*

New York: Harrison Smith and Robert Haas, Inc., 1935.
First edition, first trade printing, with dust jacket.

Presentation copy. On free front endpaper, in blue ink:

> *For Myrtle Ramey*
> *William Faulkner*
> *Oxford   Mar 26, 1935*

Accompanied by letter to Mrs. F. V. B. Demarest (Myrtle Ramey) from W. M. Reed, who secured the book and the inscription for the recipient. The letter begins as follows: "We are mailing to you today William's latest book, 'Pylon', which was released Monday and reached us yesterday. His autograph for you bears the date of yesterday, 26th, but he made the entry just a few moments ago, forgetting the true date."

169 *Pylon.*

New York: Harrison Smith and Robert Haas, Inc., 1935.
First edition, first trade printing, with dust jacket.

Presentation copy. On free front endpaper, in blue ink:

> *To Hubert Starr,*
> *god damn him*
> *Bill Faulkner*

On title page, in blue ink:

> *William Faulkner*
> *[illegible address]*
> *Los Angeles Cal*
> *William Faulkner*
> *12 Jan 1936*

170 *Pylon.*

New York: Harrison Smith and Robert Haas, Inc., 1935.
First edition, first trade printing, with dust jacket.

Presentation copy. On title page, in black ink:

> *For Malcolm Cowley*
> *William Faulkner*
> *Sherman Conn*
> *25 Oct. 1948*

171 *Pylon.*

New York: Harrison Smith and Robert Haas, Inc., 1935.
First edition, first trade printing, with dust jacket.

Fictionist, 1926–1944

172 *Pylon*.

New York: Harrison Smith and Robert Haas, Inc., 1935.
First edition, "Second Printing, March, 1935," with dust jacket.

Variant binding. Cedar cloth.

173 *Pylon*.

New York: Harrison Smith and Robert Haas, Inc., 1935.
First edition, "Second Printing, March, 1935," with dust jacket.

Variant binding. Medium blue cloth.

174 *Pylon*.

New York: Harrison Smith and Robert Haas, Inc., 1935.
First edition, "Second Printing, March, 1935," with dust jacket.

Variant binding. Turquoise blue cloth.

175 *Pylon*.

New York: Harrison Smith and Robert Haas, Inc., 1935.
First edition, "Second Printing, March, 1935," with dust jacket.

Variant binding. Mint green cloth.

176 *Pylon*.

New York: Harrison Smith and Robert Haas, Inc., 1935.
First edition, "Second Printing, March, 1935," with dust jacket.

Variant binding. White cloth.

177 *Pylon*.

New York: Harrison Smith and Robert Haas, Inc., 1935.
First edition, "Second Printing, March, 1935," with dust jacket.

Variant binding. Bright red cloth.

178 *Pylon*.

New York: Harrison Smith and Robert Haas, Inc., 1935.
First edition, "Second Printing, March, 1935," with dust jacket.

Variant binding. Redwood cloth.

179 *Pylon*.

New York: Harrison Smith and Robert Haas, Inc., 1935.
First edition, "Second Printing, March, 1935," with dust jacket.

Variant binding. Terra cotta cloth.

180 *Pylon.*

Hamburg: The Albatross Modern Continental Library, 1935.

In English. Paperback, in wrappers.

181 *Pylone.*

Paris: Gallimard, 1946.
Trans. R. N. Raimbault and Mme. G. Louis-Rousselet.
First French edition, with original glassine.

Number LIV of limited issue of 105 copies on "velin pur Lafuma Navarre."

182 "Skirmish at Sartoris."

Scribner's Magazine, 97 (April 1935), 193–200.

First publication of story which became part of *The Unvanquished*.

183 "Lion."

Harper's Magazine, 172 (December 1935), 67–77.

First publication of story later rewritten and incorporated into "The Bear" in *Go Down, Moses*.

1 9 3 6

184 Line drawing, 8½ by 11 inches, in pencil. Shows arrangement of house at 620 El Cerco Drive, Santa Monica, where Faulkners lived during one of their tenures in California.

This drawing by Faulkner (see plate 26), with penciled note at bottom by Mrs. Faulkner, was enclosed with a letter Mrs. Faulkner wrote to Malcolm Franklin, postmarked Beverly Hills, California, July 27, 1936. Stationery and envelope, which is addressed in Faulkner's hand, show imprint of "Beverly Hills Hotel and Bungalows, Beverly Hills, California."
A detailed description of this house and its setting appears in Meta Carpenter Wilde and Orin Borsten, *A Loving Gentleman*, pp. 166–175.

185 "Fool About a Horse."

Scribner's Magazine, 100 (August 1936), 80–86.

First publication of story incorporated, in revised form, into *The Hamlet*.

186 *Absalom, Absalom!*

New York: Random House, [October 26] 1936.
First edition, first printing. The limited and trade copies of this book are from the same printing.

Number 81 of signed, limited issue of 300 copies.

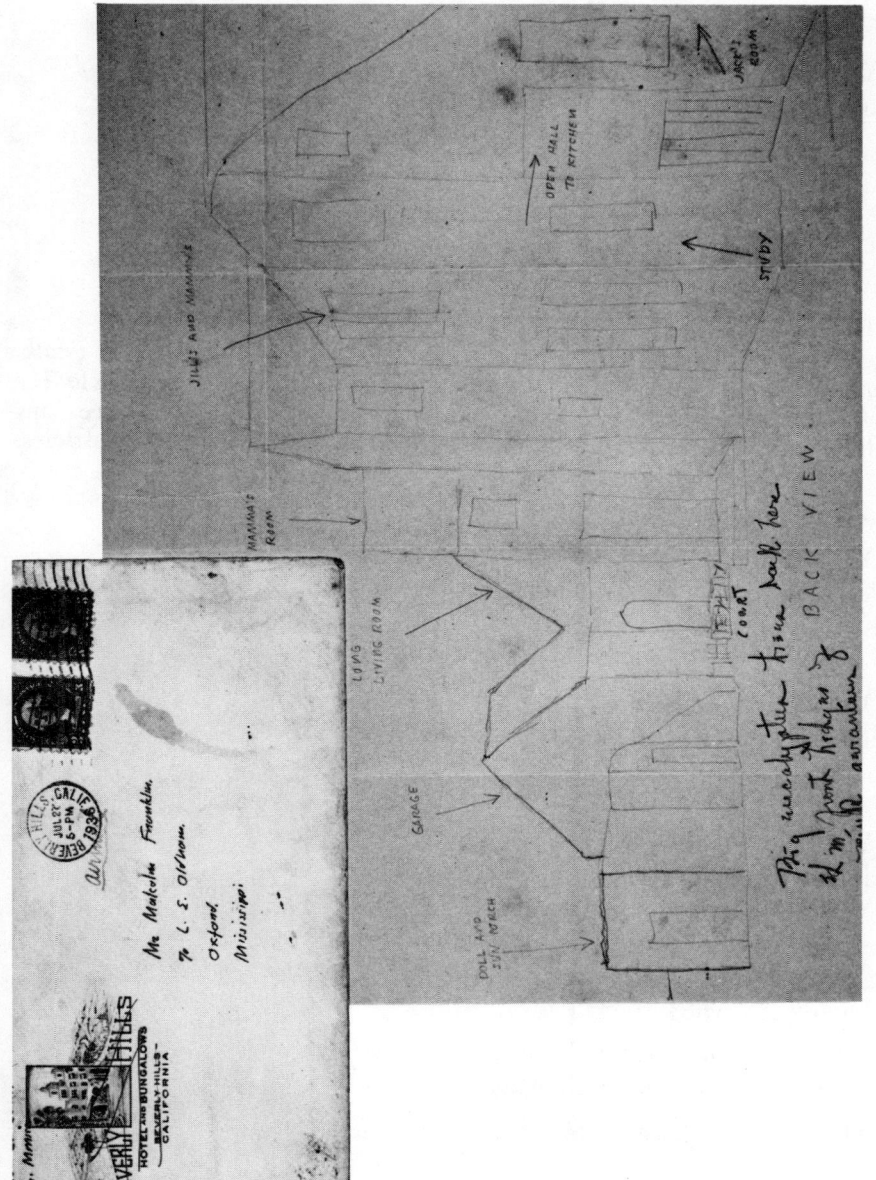

26 Faulkner's drawing of Santa Monica, California, residence, 1936

187 *Absalom, Absalom!*

New York: Random House, 1936.
First edition, first printing, with dust jacket.

Presentation copy. On title page, in black ink:

> *For Malcolm Cowley*
> *William Faulkner*
> *Sherman, Conn*
> *25 Oct. 1948*

On free front endpaper, in Cowley's hand, in pencil: "Malcolm Cowley."
Pages 31–58 of this copy have been razored out. As Cowley explains in *The Faulkner-Cowley File* (pp. 34, 47), in order to assemble a printer's copy of the materials for *The Portable Faulkner* Cowley had to mutilate some of his own Faulkner books, since many of the titles he needed were out of print and unavailable even in second-hand bookstores.

188 *Absalom, Absalom!*

New York: Random House, 1936.
First edition, first printing, with dust jacket.

189 *Absalom, Absalom!*

New York: Random House, 1936.
First edition, second printing (1936), lacking dust jacket.

190 *Absalom, Absalom!*

New York: The Modern Library, 1951.
Introduction by Harvey Breit.
First Modern Library edition (number 271), with dust jacket.

191 *Absalon! Absalon!*

Paris: Gallimard, 1953.
Trans. R.-N. Raimbault and Ch. P. Vorce.
First French edition, with original glassine.

Number 30 of limited issue of 87 copies on "velin pur fil Navarre."

192 "The Unvanquished."

The Saturday Evening Post, 209 (November 14, 1936), 12 ff.

First publication of story which became part of the *The Unvanquished*.

1938

193 *The Unvanquished*.

New York: Random House, [February 15] 1938.

Fictionist, 1926–1944

First edition, first printing. The limited and trade copies of this book are from the same printing.

Number 235 of signed, limited issue of 250 copies.
To produce *The Unvanquished* Faulkner combined a new story, "An Odor of Verbena," with six previously published ones: "Ambuscade," "Retreat," "Raid," "The Unvanquished" ("Riposte in Tertio"), "Vendée," and "Skirmish at Sartoris."

194 *The Unvanquished*.

New York: Random House, 1938.
First edition, first printing, lacking dust jacket.

Presentation copy. On free front endpaper, in black ink:

> *To Phil Stone,*
> *from William Faulkner*
> *Oxford, Miss.*
> *20 Jany 1938*

195 *The Unvanquished*.

New York: Random House, 1938.
First edition, first printing, with dust jacket.

196 *The Unvanquished*.

New York: Random House, 1938.
First edition, second printing, with dust jacket.

Presentation copy. On title page, in black ink:

> *For Malcolm Cowley*
> *William Faulkner*
> *Sherman, Conn*
> *25 Oct. 1948*

On free front endpaper, in Cowley's hand, in pencil: "Malcolm Cowley / Aug 1945."

197 *The Unvanquished*.

New York: The New American Library, 1959.
Foreword by Carvel Collins.
First Signet Classics edition (CD9), August 1959, paperback.

Inscribed by Collins to Brodsky.
See also item **421**.

198 *L'invaincu*.

Paris: Gallimard, 1949.
Trans. R. N. Raimbault and Ch.-P. Vorce.
First French edition, with original glassine.

Number XLI of limited issue of 205 copies on "vélin pur fil Lafuma Navarre."

199 Photograph, 5 by 7 inches, with matting and cardboard frame. Shows Faulkner family and guests at hunt breakfast, Rowan Oak, May 8, 1938.

On verso Estelle Faulkner has listed the names of all the guests. Verso also shows the imprint of "Cofield Studios / Oxford, Mississippi."
Copy belonged to 'Bama McLean.
Segment of this photograph reproduced in Blotner, *Faulkner: A Biography*, p. 992.

1 9 3 9

200 *The Wild Palms*.

New York: Random House, [January 19] 1939.
First edition, first printing. The limited and trade copies of this book are from the same printing.

Number 236 of signed, limited issue of 250 copies.

201 *The Wild Palms*.

New York: Random House, 1939.
First edition, first printing, with dust jacket.

Presentation copy. On free front endpaper, in black ink:

> *Vance C Broach.*
> *from his kinsman,*
> *William Faulkner*

On title page, in black ink:

> *William Faulkner*
> *Oxford, Miss*
> *30 March, 1941*

202 *The Wild Palms*.

New York: Random House, 1939.
First edition, first printing, in wrappers.

Advance review copy.

203 *The Wild Palms*.

New York: Random House, 1939.
First edition, first printing, with dust jacket.

204 *The Wild Palms*.

London: Chatto & Windus, 1939.
First British edition, first printing, with dust jacket.

Fictionist, 1926–1944

Presentation copy. On free front endpaper, in blue ink:

> *To Malcolm Franklin*
>
> > William Faulkner
> > Oxford, Miss
> > 20 March 1946

On title page, in blue ink:

> *William Faulkner*

205 *Les palmiers sauvages.*

Paris: Gallimard, 1952.
Trans. with preface by M.-E. Coindreau.
First French edition, with original glassine.

Number 46 of limited issue of 107 copies on "vélin pur fil Lafuma-Navarre."

206 "Barn Burning."

Harper's Magazine, 179 (June 1939), 86–96.

First publication of the story which became, in condensed form, a part of *The Hamlet*.

1940

207 Last will and testament of William Faulkner, dated March 27, 1940. Signed carbon typescript, 6 pages, 14 by 8½ inches, watermarked "VALID ONION SKIN."

Includes, in both Faulkner's and Phil Stone's hands, penciled changes entered when Faulkner revised his will in 1951. Signed and dated on each page, in brown ink, "William Faulkner / 3/27/40." See plate 27.

This document, prepared for Faulkner by Stone, includes Faulkner's provision for Ned Barnett, the black man who had faithfully served four generations of the Faulkner family. See Robert W. Hamblin, "Lucas Beauchamp, Ned Barnett, and William Faulkner's 1940 Will," *Studies in Bibliography*, 32 (1979), 281–283.

208 *The Hamlet.*

Carbon typescript, with numerous holographic corrections by Faulkner. Two volumes (pp. 1–329, 330–582), bound in brown boards. Typed on cover label of each volume: "First Carbon Copy of / original type-written manuscript of / THE HAMLET / By William Faulkner."

Presentation copy. On page 1, in black ink (see plate 28):

> *To My Godson, Philip Alston Stone*
> > *may he be faithful*
> > > *fortunate, and brave*

Item 11.

My brother, ~~John Falkner,~~ and his descendants are to have the use of the farm Northeast of Oxford which I now own, rent free, and use of all equipment and livestock on it necessary for working said farm, free of charge. However, my Executors and Testamentary Guardians shall have full right to sell said farm and all equipment and livestock at any time they consider in their judgment such sale to be necessary for the well-being of my other legatees. My brother, John Falkner, is to have the first option to purchase all of said property at a purchase price to be fixed as near as possible in accordance with what my brother, John Falkner, can pay. This option is to expire when my Executors and Testamentary Guardians think it advisable to sell said property or, in any event, it shall expire when my daughter, Jill Falkner, becomes of legal age. If said property, or any part thereof, has not been sold when my daughter, Jill Faulkner, becomes of legal age, then all of said property shall go to my daughter, Jill Faulkner. In the event my brother, ~~John~~ Falkner, shall exercise his option to purchase said property, he shall be credited on such purchase price with the value of all improvements made by him and all taxes paid by him from the time of my death until the exercise by him of such option but if he does not exercise such option, he shall not recover for any such improvements made or taxes paid. The above devise is made with the understanding that Ned Barnett, colored, if he outlives me, is to have the house he now lives in, rent free, as long as he remains on this farm. If at my death the title to said farm is clear in my name, the said ~~Barnett is to receive clear title~~ to said house and the piece of ground on which it rests ~~and the line between his property and the other property is to be established by my Executors and Testamentary Guardians and is not to infringe upon other buildings.~~ The said Ned Barnett is also to have rent free to cultivate a five-acre piece of ground to be selected by my Executors and Testamentary Guardians and is to have

27 Page of Faulkner's 1940 will, with revisions made in 1951

BOOK ONE
FLEM
~~PEASANTS~~
~~BOOK ONE~~
Chapter One

Section I

To My Godson, Philip Alston Stone
May he be faithful
humble, and brave

William Faulkner
Xmas 1945
Oxford, Miss

1.

Frenchman's Bend was a section of rich river-bottom country lying twenty miles southeast of Jefferson. Hill-cradled and remote, definite yet without boundaries, straddling into two counties and owning allegiance to neither, it had been the original grant and site of a tremendous pre-Civil War plantation, the ruins of which——the gutted shell of an enormous house with its fallen stables and slave quarters and overgrown gardens and brick terraces and promenades——were still known as the Old Frenchman's place, although the original boundaries now existed only on old faded records in the Chancery Clerk's office in the county court house in Jefferson, and even some of the once-fertile fields had long since reverted to the cane-and-cypress jungle from which their first master had hewed them.

He hadquite possibly been a foreigner, though not necessarily French, since to the people who had come after him and had almost obliterated all trace of his sojourn, anyone speaking the tongue with a foreign flavor or whose appearance or even occupation was strange, would have been a Frenchman regardless of what nationality he might affirm, just as to their more urban co-evals (if he had elected to

1.

28 Page 1 of typescript version of *The Hamlet*. Inscribed to Faulkner's godson, Philip Alston Stone.

> William Faulkner
> Xmas 1945
> Oxford, Miss

On page 329, in black ink:

> William Faulkner

On page 330, in black ink:

> To Philip, my godson
> William Faulkner

On page 582, in black ink:

> William Faulkner
> Xmas 1945
> Oxford, Miss

The inscription on page 1 echoes the words of "Little sister Death" to the protagonist of *Mayday* (p. 43): "Rise, Sir Galwyn; be faithful, fortunate, and brave."

209 *The Hamlet.*

Uncorrected galley proof. Galleys 1–150. Stapled and bound in manila boards with black tape on spine.

Label on cover reads: "UNCORRECTED PROOF from RANDOM HOUSE. 20 EAST 57 STREET. N.Y. / TITLE THE HAMLET / AUTHOR WILLIAM FAULKNER / DATE OF PUBLICATION APRIL 1, 1940 / PRICE $2.50."

210 *The Hamlet.*

New York: Random House, [April 1] 1940.
First edition, first printing, with original glassine. The limited and trade copies of this book are from the same printing.

Number 38 of signed, limited issue of 250 copies.
Faulkner incorporated several short stories into the text of *The Hamlet*: "Spotted Horses," "The Hound," "Lizards in Jamshyd's Courtyard," "Fool About a Horse," "Barn Burning," and "Afternoon of a Cow." All except the last had previous publication.

211 *The Hamlet.*

New York: Random House, 1940.
First edition, first printing, lacking dust jacket.

Dedication page reads: "To Phil Stone."
Presentation copy which, according to Emily Stone, was given to Phil Stone to replace his inscribed copy destroyed by fire in 1942. On free front endpaper, in black ink (see plate 35):

> To Phil Stone
> *from Bill*

On title page, in black ink:

Fictionist, 1926–1944

William Faulkner
4 Feb. 1946

212 *The Hamlet.*

New York: Random House, 1940.
First edition, first printing, with dust jacket.

Advance review copy inscribed on free front endpaper, in black ink: "George Marion O'Donnell." Laid in is review slip, verso of which contains penciled notes by O'Donnell, the critic whose 1939 essay entitled "Faulkner's Mythology" was one of the first treatments of Faulkner's work as a unified whole.

213 *The Hamlet.*

New York: Random House, 1940.
First edition, first printing, with dust jacket.

Back of jacket lists other Random House titles. Yellow Random House bookmark laid in.

214 *The Hamlet.*

New York: Random House, 1940.
First edition, first printing, with dust jacket.

Back of jacket displays excerpts from reviews of *The Hamlet*. Yellow Random House bookmark laid in.

215 *The Hamlet.*

New York: Random House, 1940.
First edition, second printing, lacking dust jacket.

216 *The Hamlet.*

New York: Random House, [1956].
Second American edition, probably reprint, with dust jacket.

Presentation copy given to Malcolm Franklin. On free front endpaper, in black ink:

> *To Buddy, with love*
> *Pappy*
> 3 Dec 1960

On title page, in black ink:

> *William Faulkner*

217 *The Hamlet.*

New York: Random House, [1956].
Second American edition, probably reprint, with dust jacket.

218 *The Hamlet*.

London: Chatto & Windus, 1940.
First British edition, first printing, lacking dust jacket.

Presentation copy. On free front endpaper, in black ink:

> *To my son,*
> *Malcolm Franklin*
> *William Faulkner*
> *Oxford, Miss*
> *20 March 1946*

On title page, in blue ink:

> *William Faulkner*

Also on free front endpaper, in Franklin's hand, in blue and black ink: "Malcolm A Franklin / M A Franklin / ['Rowan Oak' *del.*] / Oxford, Mississippi / 29 X State Street / Charleston, S.C."

219 *Le hameau*.

Paris: Gallimard, 1959.
Trans. René Hilleret.
First French edition, with original glassine.

Unnumbered S.P. copy.

220 *Le hameau*.

Paris: Gallimard, 1959.
Trans. René Hilleret.
First French edition, with original glassine.

Number 1 of limited issue of 66 copies on "vélin pur fil Lafuma-Navarre."

221 "A Point of Law."

Collier's, 105 (June 22, 1940), 20ff.

First publication of story revised and incorporated into *Go Down, Moses* as first section of "The Fire and the Hearth."

222 Disney, Dorothy Cameron. *The Balcony*. New York: Random House, 1940. First edition, first printing, lacking dust jacket.

Inscribed by Faulkner. On free front endpaper, in blue ink:

> *William Faulkner*
> *Rowan Oak*
> *August 1940*

This book, which Faulkner had given to Malcolm Franklin, is not listed in Blotner, comp., *William Faulkner's Library*.

223 "The Old People."

Harper's Magazine, 181 (September 1940), 418–425.

First publication of story which became, in revised form, part of *Go Down, Moses*.

224 "Pantaloon in Black."

Harper's Magazine, 181 (October 1940), 503–513.

First publication of story which was slightly revised and incorporated into *Go Down, Moses*.

225 "Gold Is Not Always."

Atlantic Monthly, 166 (November 1940), 563–570.

First publication of story revised and incorporated into *Go Down, Moses* as section two of "The Fire and the Hearth."

226 Hooton, Earnest Albert. *Twilight of Man*. New York: G. P. Putnam's Sons, 1939. First edition, first printing, lacking dust jacket.

Front paste-down contains book plate of Malcolm Argyll Franklin and initials "M. A. F."

Inscribed by Faulkner as Christmas gift to Franklin. On free front endpaper, in black ink:

> *Malcolm A. Franklin*
> *from Mama & Billy*
> *Xmas. 1940*

1941

227 "Go Down, Moses."

Collier's, 107 (January 25, 1941), 19ff.

First publication of story which subsequently became the title story of *Go Down, Moses*.

228 Canceled check payable to Faulkner and signed "Mrs. Phil Stone," dated August 25, 1941. On Bank of Oxford, for $25.00. Endorsed "William Faulkner" on August 29, 1941.

Installment on personal loan Faulkner had made to Stone.

1942

229 "The Bear."

The Saturday Evening Post, 214 (May 9, 1942), 30ff.

    Different version of story that appears in *Go Down, Moses*. Omits section 4.

230 "Delta Autumn."

Story, 20 (May–June 1942), 46–55.

    Different version of story that appears in *Go Down, Moses*.

231 *Go Down, Moses and Other Stories*.

New York: Random House, [May 11] 1942.
First edition, first printing. The limited and trade copies of this book are from the same printing.

    Number 28 of signed, limited issue of 100 copies.
    Of the seven stories which comprise *Go Down, Moses*, only "Was" and portions of "The Fire and the Hearth" had not been previously published. The other stories represent reworkings of material which had appeared earlier as "Lion," "The Old People," "Pantaloon in Black," "Gold Is Not Always," "Go Down, Moses," "A Point of Law," and "Delta Autumn."

232 *Go Down, Moses and Other Stories*.

New York: Random House, 1942.
First edition, first printing, with dust jacket.

    Presumably first state of binding. Black cloth stamped on front and spine in red and gold. Top edge stained red.
    Presentation copy. On free front endpaper, in blue-black ink:

> *Phil Stone, from Bill*

On title page, in blue-black ink:

> *William Faulkner*
> *Oxford, Miss*
> *24 March, 1942*

    Also on free front endpaper, in Stone's hand, in blue-black ink: "Phil Stone / Phil Stone / Oxford, Mississippi / March 24, 1942."

233 *Go Down, Moses and Other Stories*.

New York: Random House, 1942.
First edition, first printing, with dust jacket.

    Presumably first state of binding.
    Presentation copy given to 'Bama McLean. On free front endpaper, in blue ink:

Fictionist, 1926–1944

For Aunt Bama
with love

William Faulkner
Oxford, Miss
28 Nov 1947

234 *Go Down, Moses and Other Stories.*

New York: Random House, 1942.
First edition, first printing, with dust jacket.

Presumably first state of binding.
Presentation copy. On title page, in black ink:

For Muriel Cowley
a charming & delightful lady
with gratitude

William Faulkner
Sherman, Conn
25 Oct. 1948

On free front endpaper, in Malcolm Cowley's hand, in pencil: "Malcolm Cowley."
Book also contains penciled notations by Malcolm Cowley throughout text.

235 *Go Down, Moses and Other Stories.*

New York: Random House, 1942.
First edition, first printing, with dust jacket.

Presumably first state of binding.

236 *Go Down, Moses and Other Stories.*

New York: Random House, 1942.
First edition, first printing, with dust jacket.

Variant binding. Tile red cloth stamped on spine only in green. Edges unstained.

237 *Go Down, Moses and Other Stories.*

New York: Random House, 1942.
First edition, first printing, lacking dust jacket.

Variant binding. Ivory cloth stamped on spine only in green. Edges unstained.

238 *Go Down, Moses, and Other Stories.*

London: Chatto & Windus, 1942.
First British edition, first printing, with dust jacket.

239 *Descends, Moïse.*

Paris: Gallimard, 1955.
Trans. R.-N. Raimbault.
First French edition, with original glassine.

Number 54 of limited issue of 76 copies on "vélin pur fil Lafuma-Navarre."

240 Daniel, Robert W. *A Catalogue of the Writings of William Faulkner*. New Haven: Yale University Library, 1942.

Issued to accompany a Faulkner exhibit at Yale University, Summer 1942.
Copy belonged to Phil Stone. Inscribed on cover, in blue ink, "Phil Stone / Oxford / Mississippi"; on title page, in blue ink, "Phil Stone / Oxford, Mississippi / July 21, 1942"; and on page 19, in blue ink, "Phil Stone."

241 Daniel, Robert W. *A Catalogue of the Writings of William Faulkner*. New Haven: Yale University Library, 1942.

Inscribed by Daniel on title page, in blue ink: "For L. D. Brodsky, who has far / outdistanced me as a Faulkner / collector and bibliographer—— / Robert W. Daniel / [rule] / Gambier, Ohio / 18 Nov. 1978."

242 Group of materials relating to Faulkner exhibit at Yale University Library, Summer 1942.

Includes Robert Daniel's handwritten notes treating materials in the exhibit, 10 pages, 11 by 8½ inches, and the following letters concerning Faulkner and the exhibit:

a. Ben F. Wasson, Sr., to Daniel, March 16, 1942, signed ribbon typescript, 1 page.

b. Phil Stone to Daniel, April 6, 1942, signed ribbon typescript, 2 pages.

Contains information about *The Marble Faun*, Faulkner's military experiences, and Stone's judgments of Faulkner as a writer.

c. Stone to Daniel, April 25, 1942, signed ribbon typescript, 2 pages.

d. Stone to Daniel, May 12, 1942, signed ribbon typescript, 1 page.

e. Daniel to Mrs. Walter McLean, July 4, 1942, signed ribbon typescript, 2 pages (1 leaf).

f. Daniel to Estelle Lake, July 4, 1942, signed ribbon typescript, 1 page.

g. Daniel to Mrs. McLean, July 15, 1942, holograph, 2 pages (1 leaf).

h. James T. Babb to Mrs. McLean, October 21, 1942, signed ribbon typescript, 1 page.

IV

THE LATE YEARS

Laureate

1945–1962

I feel that this award was not made to me as a man, but to my work—a life's work in the agony and sweat of the human spirit, not for glory and least of all for profit, but to create out of the materials of the human spirit something which did not exist before.
—*Nobel Prize Acceptance Speech*

The Portable FAULKNER

Edited by Malcolm Cowley

For Malcolm Cowley
William Faulkner
[illegible]
25 Feb 1948

THE VIKING PRESS • NEW YORK
1946

29 Title page of *The Portable Faulkner* which Faulkner inscribed for Malcolm Cowley

IV

THE LATE YEARS: *Laureate*

By 1945 William Faulkner had produced thirteen novels, two collections of stories (plus two other books of single short stories), and two volumes of poetry. He held membership in the National Institute of Arts and Letters, and he was generally recognized among fellow authors as a writer of extraordinary talent and achievement. Yet, as Malcolm Cowley has noted, Faulkner was virtually unknown to the vast majority of the American reading public. In France, even at this early date, Faulkner was, in the words of Jean Paul Sartre, "a god"; but in his own country all of his books except one—the notorious *Sanctuary*—were out of print.

Cowley thought such neglect of an outstanding twentieth-century novelist was unfortunate. Having read and reviewed for the *New Republic* several of Faulkner's works, Cowley sensed a pattern and a significance in Faulkner's work deserving of popular attention and serious critical study. Convinced of Faulkner's importance, Cowley persuaded Viking Press to allow him to put together a representative collection of Faulkner's fiction. The result was *The Portable Faulkner*, completed with Faulkner's endorsement and assistance and published in 1946.

It would be an exaggeration, of course, to say that Malcolm Cowley "discovered" William Faulkner and that *The Portable Faulkner* "made" Faulkner's literary reputation. Still, Cowley's book came at a propitious time and did much to make Faulkner's work available to the public and respectable to the critics. Needless to say, Cowley's judgment that Faulkner's work deserved such attention was vindicated beyond all doubt four years later when Faulkner was awarded the Nobel Prize for Literature.

The winning of the Nobel Prize robbed Faulkner of much of the privacy which he had always so jealously guarded. Though never comfortable with his new role as public figure, to his credit Faulkner accepted the responsibilities which he felt the Prize required of him. He made goodwill trips abroad on behalf of the Department of State; he lectured to college audiences and public gatherings; he accepted an appointment as writer-in-residence at the University of Virginia. Most significantly, he took a strong stand—frequently in the form of press releases and letters to editors—in support of civil rights for Negroes during the troubled early years of integration in the South.

Fortunately, however, Faulkner the public figure did not displace Faulkner the writer. During the late years Faulkner continued to produce impressive, if hardly great, fiction. *Intruder in the Dust* (1948), one of only two or three Faulkner works converted into successful movies, combined "whodunit" murder suspense with strong civil rights pronouncements. *Requiem for a Nun* (1951), a novel in the form of a play, demonstrated Faulkner's abiding obsession with technical innovation. *A Fable* (1954), a retelling of the Christ story, overcame mixed reviews to earn for Faulkner a Pulitzer Prize. *The Town* (1957) and *The Mansion* (1959) successfully rounded out the Snopes trilogy. And *The Reivers*, published only one month before Faulkner succumbed to a heart attack on July 6, 1962, proved that only death, and not a loss of his creative genius, had brought Faulkner to that point to which he had frequently alluded, when "I shall break the pencil and . . . have to stop."

1945

243 Cowley, Malcolm. "William Faulkner Revisited." *Saturday Review of Literature*, 28 (April 14, 1945), 13–16.

First publication of portion of long essay which became basis for introduction to *The Portable Faulkner*.
Inscribed by Cowley to Brodsky.

244 Letter from Phil Stone to Malcolm Cowley, dated April 30, 1945, unsigned carbon typescript, 2 pages.

Takes issue with several of Cowley's statements in *Saturday Review* article of April 14.

1946

245 *The Portable Faulkner.*
New York: The Viking Press, [April 29] 1946.
Ed. with introduction by Malcolm Cowley.
First edition, first printing, with dust jacket.

Top and side edge unstained; bottom edge stained blue.
Presentation copy. On free front endpaper, in blue ink:

> *Vance Carter Broach*
> *from his cousin,*
> *William Faulkner*

On title page, in blue ink:

MALCOLM COWLEY
SHERMAN, CONN. 06784

August 1975.

This beat-up copy of *The Portable Faulkner* is the one I used for many years in teaching and lecturing. Faulkner autographed it for me when he was at our house in 1948. It is first edition, first printing. It traveled with me to the University of Washington, 1950, Stanford, 1956, 59, 61, 65, Minnesota, 1971, the University of Warwick, 1973, and other campuses. Sometimes I made notes in the margins. When the lavender dust jacket wore out, I mended it with Scotch tape. The book deserves an honorable retirement; give the old racehorse plenty of oats and hay and a warm stall.

Malcolm Cowley

30   Provenance paper for Malcolm Cowley's personal copy of *The Portable Faulkner*

William Faulkner
Oxford, Miss
28 Nov 1947

246   *The Portable Faulkner.*

New York: The Viking Press, 1946.
Ed. with introduction by Malcolm Cowley.
First edition, first printing, with dust jacket.

> Edges unstained.
> Presentation copy (see plates 29 and 30). On title page, in blue ink:
>
>> *For Malcolm Cowley*
>> *William Faulkner*
>> *Sherman Conn*
>> *25 Oct. 1948*

This copy was Cowley's working copy and contains his marginal notations throughout.

247   *The Portable Faulkner.*

New York: The Viking Press, 1946.
Ed. with introduction by Malcolm Cowley.
First edition, first printing, lacking dust jacket.

> Edges unstained.
> Copy given by Faulkner to Phil Stone.

248   *The Portable Faulkner.*

New York: The Viking Press, 1946.
Ed. with introduction by Malcolm Cowley.
First edition, first printing, with dust jacket.

> Edges stained blue.
> Inscribed by Cowley to Brodsky.

249   *The Portable Faulkner.*

New York: The Viking Press, 1946.
Ed. with introduction by Malcolm Cowley.
First edition, second printing (October 1949), with dust jacket.

> Edges stained blue-gray.
> Inscribed by Cowley to Brodsky.

250   *The Indispensable Faulkner.*

New York: The Book Society, 1950.
Ed. with introduction by Malcolm Cowley.
First edition, reprint, with glassine, lacking original slip case.

THE SOUND AND THE FURY

Malcolm Cowley

To Malcolm Cowley

Who beat me to what
was to have been the
leisurely pleasure of my
old age.

William Faulkner

31 Half title page of *The Sound and the Fury* which Faulkner inscribed to Malcolm Cowley

Same contents as *The Portable Faulkner*.
Copy belonged to Myrtle Ramey Demarest. Inscribed by Cowley to Brodsky.

251 *664 pagine di William Faulkner.*

Milan: Il Saggiatore, 1959.
Trans. Edoardo Bizzarri and others.
First edition, with dust jacket.

Italian translation of *The Portable Faulkner*, with the addition of two excerpts from *Requiem for a Nun*.
Copy belonged to Malcolm Cowley. Inscribed by Cowley to Brodsky.

252 *The Sound and the Fury & As I Lay Dying.*

New York: The Modern Library, [December 20] 1946.
First joint edition, presumably first printing, with dust jacket.

Presentation copy. On half title page, in blue ink:

> *For Vance Carter Broach*
> *from his cousin*
> *William Faulkner*

On title page, in blue ink:

> *William Faulkner*
> *Oxford, Miss*
> *28 Nov 1947*

253 *The Sound and the Fury & As I Lay Dying.*

New York: The Modern Library, 1946.
First joint edition, presumably first printing, with dust jacket.

1947

254 "Afternoon of a Cow."

Furioso, 2 (Summer 1947), 5–17.

"By Ernest V. Trueblood" (pseudonym). First English language publication of story which appears in revised form as part of *The Hamlet*.

255 Tate, Allen, ed. *A Southern Vanguard*. New York: Prentice Hall, Inc., 1947. First edition, first printing, with dust jacket.

Reprints Malcolm Cowley's article, "William Faulkner's Legend of the South," which is inscribed by Cowley to Brodsky.

1948

256 *Intruder in the Dust.*

New York: Random House, [September 27] 1948.
First edition, first printing, with dust jacket.

Presentation copy given to Phil Stone. On free front endpaper, in blue-black ink:

> *To Phil*
> *from Bill*
> 27 Sept 1948

On title page, in blue-black ink:

> *William Faulkner*
> *Oxford, Miss*
> *27 Sept 1948*

Also on free front endpaper, in Stone's hand, in blue-black ink: "Phil & Emily Stone / Oxford, Mississippi / Sept 27, 1948. / Two days after Bill's 51st / birthday."

This copy contains Stone's characteristic marginal notations, in pencil, throughout. On last page of text, p. 247, Stone has written, in blue ink:

A skillful job, Bill, but it seems too trickey [*sic*] in places and there is too damned much talk in it.

(For Philip and Araminta)   This tale grew out of a suggestion I made to Bill and he wrote it in six weeks to sell to the slicks because he needed money and the slicks rejected it. Then MGM bought it for fifty thousand dollars and made a movie of it. The premiere will be here Tuesday week, Oct 11, and Mother and Philip and I are going (Araminta is just ten months old).

Finished at home Oct 2 (Sunday night) 1949.

257 *Intruder in the Dust.*

New York: Random House, 1948.
First edition, first printing, lacking dust jacket.

Presentation copy given to Malcolm Franklin. On free front endpaper, in blue ink:

> *Buddy, from Pappy*
> *Rowan Oak*
> *29 Sept 1948*

On title page, in blue ink:

> *William Faulkner*
> *Oxford, Miss*
> *29 Sept 1948*

On front paste-down, in Franklin's hand, in blue-black ink: "M A Franklin / 29 Sept. '48" and "M. Argyle Franklin / D. of Biophysics / U. of M. Med. Center / Jackson, Miss."

258 *Intruder in the Dust.*

New York: Random House, 1948.
First edition, first printing, with dust jacket.

Presentation copy. On free front endpaper, in blue ink:

> *For Mrs. Calvin Brown*
> *Bill Faulkner*

> *For Edith*
> *Xmas 1948*
> *Bill Faulkner*

On title page, in blue ink:

> *William Faulkner*
> *Oxford Miss*
> *10 Dec 1948*

259 *Intruder in the Dust.*

New York: Random House, 1948.
First edition, first printing, with dust jacket.

260 *Intruder in the Dust.*

New York: Random House, 1948.
First edition, second printing [ca. 1948], lacking dust jacket.

Presentation copy. On front flyleaf, in blue ink:

> *for Jim Devine*
> *Bill Faulkner*

On title page, in blue ink:

> *William Faulkner*
> *New York*
> *30 Oct. 1948*

261 *Intruder in the Dust.*

New York: Random House, 1948.
First edition, second printing [ca. 1948], with dust jacket.

Inscribed copy which belonged to Myrtle Ramey Demarest. On title page, in blue ink:

> *William Faulkner*
> *Oxford, Miss*
> *29 Jan 1952*

262 *Intruder in the Dust.*

Omnibook, 11 (December 1948), 89–129.

An abridgment.

263 *L'intrus.*

Paris: Gallimard, 1952.
Trans. R.-N. Raimbault.
First French edition, with original glassine.

Number 68 of limited issue of 131 copies on "vélin pur fil des Papeteries Lafuma-Navarre."

264 "The Wishing-Tree."

Ribbon typescript, 44 pages, stapled and bound in manila boards with brown tape on spine. Typed on the cover: "THE WISHING-TREE / BY / WILLIAM FAULKNER."

This copy, the text of which differs significantly from the published version, was one of two (the other was given to Ruth Ford's daughter) which Faulkner copied in 1948 from the version of the story he had presented to Dr. Calvin Brown's daughter in 1927.
Presentation copy. On page 1, in blue ink (see plate 32):

> *For Philip Stone II,*
> *from his god-father.*
> *William Faulkner*
> *Oxford.*
> *Xmas 1948*

1949

265 "William Faulkner's Legend of the South." Leaflet for lecture by Malcolm Cowley, University of Virginia, May 6, 1949.

Reprints brief excerpt from introduction to *The Portable Faulkner*.
Inscribed by Cowley to Brodsky.

266 *The Oxford Eagle*, Thursday, October 6, 1949. Banner headline reads: "World Premiere Excitement Ready To Break."

Contains stories about the upcoming premiere of the Faulkner novel-turned-film, *Intruder in the Dust*.
Copy 'Bama McLean mailed to Vance Broach. At top of page 1 Mrs. McLean has written: "Better pictures / of Billie—& / 'write-ups'— / see all / pages—"

267 Program brochure for world premiere of movie, *Intruder in the Dust*. Lyric Theatre, Oxford, Mississippi, 8:00 P.M., Tuesday, October 11, 1949. Eight pages.

Copy belonged to Phil Stone (cf. Stone's notation in item **256**).

For Philip Stone II.
from his god-father.
William Faulkner
Oxford.
Xmas 1948

THE WISHING-TREE

She was still asleep, but she could feel herself rising up out of sleep just like a balloon: it was like she was a goldfish in a round bowl of sleep, rising and rising through the warm waters of sleep, to the top. And then she would be awake.

And so she was awake, but she didn't open her eyes at once. Instead, she lay quite still and warm in her bed, and it was like there was another little balloon inside her, getting bigger and bigger and rising and rising. Soon it would be at her mouth, then it would pop out and jump up against the ceiling as though it were laughing at her. The little balloon inside her got bigger and bigger, making all her body and her arms and legs tingle, as if she had just eaten peppermint. What can it be? she wondered, keeping her eyes shut tight, trying to remember from yesterday. What can it be?

'It's your birthday," a voice said near her, and her eyes flew open. There, standing beside the bed, was a strange boy with a thin ugly face and hair so red that it made a glow in the room. He wore a black velvet suit with red stockings and

1.

32 Page 1 of typescript version of *The Wishing Tree*. Inscribed by Faulkner to Philip Stone.

Laureate, 1945–1962

268 *Knight's Gambit.*

Uncorrected galley proof. Galleys 1–75A. Tied in blue paper covers with yellow label printed in black.

Label reads: "Uncorrected Proof from / Random House / for ADVANCE readers." Stamped in red on front cover: "FILE COPY / PLEASE RETURN TO / PUBLICITY DEPARTMENT / RANDOM HOUSE, INC."

269 *Knight's Gambit.*

New York: Random House, [November 7] 1949.
First edition, first printing, with dust jacket.

Presentation copy given to Malcolm Franklin. On free front endpaper, in blue-black ink:

>*Buddy, on his birthday. 1949*
>*Pappy*

On title page, in blue-black ink:

>*William Faulkner*
>*Oxford, Miss*
>*3 Dec 1949*

Knight's Gambit includes six stories: "Smoke," "Monk," "Hand Upon the Waters," "Tomorrow," "An Error in Chemistry," and "Knight's Gambit." Only the title story had not been published previously.

270 *Knight's Gambit.*

New York: Random House, 1949.
First edition, first printing, with dust jacket.

Copy belonged to Phil Stone. Inscribed by Stone on free front endpaper, in blue ink: "Phil and Emily Stone / Oxford, Mississippi / Dec. 17, 1949."
Contains Stone's characteristic marginal notations throughout text. On page 246, the concluding page of the title story, Stone has written, in blue ink:

>A damned good job, Bill. Far and away the best thing in the book.
>Finished in the little house (living room) Sunday night, January 1, 1950, with Emily sitting here reading a brief of mine, Philip singing in the bath-tub and Araminta sound asleep in the front bedroom.

271 *Knight's Gambit.*

New York: Random House, 1949.
First edition, first printing, with dust jacket.

272 *Le gambit du cavalier.*

Paris: Gallimard, 1951.
Trans. André du Bouchet.
First French edition, with original glassine.

Number 55 of limited issue of 129 copies on "vélin pur fil des Papeteries Lafuma-Navarre."

1950

273 Correspondence between Phil Stone and Carvel Collins, dated April-May, 1950, regarding a proposed *Life* magazine article on Faulkner.

a. Collins to Stone, April 28, 1950, signed ribbon typescript, 2 pages.

Collins noted that he had received a proposal from *Life* for a critical-biographical piece on Faulkner. Collins expressed considerable interest in the project but indicated he would insist on having final approval over the contents of the article. He requested Stone's advice and assistance.

b. Stone to Collins, April 28 [sic], 1950, unsigned carbon typescript, 2 pages.

Stone encouraged Collins to do the piece but added: "If there is anything in the world I do not want to do it is commercialize on my friendship with Bill, one of the finest things in my whole life." Stone further noted that he would talk to Faulkner about the matter.

c. Collins to Stone, May 1, 1950, signed ribbon typescript, 1 page.

Collins assured Stone that there would be no invasion of Faulkner's privacy—"no interviews, no requests for the name of his breakfast food, and by all means no photographers taking pictures in his home."

d. Stone to Collins, May 3, 1950, unsigned carbon typescript, 2 pages.

e. Stone to Collins, May 8, 1950, unsigned carbon typescript, 2 pages.

Stone informed Collins that Faulkner was upset about the proposed article and wanted, if possible, to prevent its being done. Stone quoted Faulkner as saying that Malcolm Cowley had wanted to write a similar article but had agreed at Faulkner's urging not to do it.

f. Western Union telegram, Collins to Stone, May 15, 1950.

It reads: "IF MR FAULKNER WANTS KNOW [sic] LIFE MAGAZINE ARTICLE THERE SHOULD BE NONE. I HAVE WRITTEN LIFE SO BEST WISHES=CARVEL="

Robert Coughlan subsequently accepted the *Life* assignment, and his article appeared in two parts ("The Private World of William Faulkner" and "The Man Behind the Faulkner Myth") in the September 28 and October 5, 1953, issues of *Life*. Faulkner, greatly disturbed by what he thought was an invasion of privacy and an infringement upon individual rights, reflected upon the incident in his essay, "On Privacy: The American Dream: What Happened to It," *Harper's Magazine*, 211 (July 1955), 33–38.

274 *Collected Stories of William Faulkner.*

New York: Random House, [August 21] 1950.
First edition, first printing, with dust jacket.

Gray cloth. Lettering on spine stamped in gold on blue background. Top edge stained gray-blue. Article "The" added to title on spine.
Presentation copy. On free front endpaper, in blue-black ink:

> *To Phil Stone.*
> *from Bill Faulkner*

On title page, in blue-black ink:

> *William Faulkner*
> *Oxford, Miss*
> *20 Aug 1950*

On free front endpaper, in Stone's hand, in blue-black ink: "Phil & Emily Stone / Oxford, Miss. / August 27, 1950. / Araminta, Philip & I drove down to Bill's / house and got this book on Sunday morning."
This volume includes forty-two stories, all of which had been previously published.

275 *Collected Stories of William Faulkner.*

New York: Random House, 1950.
First edition, first printing, with dust jacket.

Inscribed copy. On title page, in blue ink:

> *William Faulkner*

Inscribed on front paste-down by Malcolm Franklin. In black ink: "Malcolm A. Franklin / Jackson, Miss." Beneath that, in blue ink: "Rowan Oak / Oxford, Miss." Beneath that, in red pencil: "46 Queen St. / or / Room 405 Res. Bld. / Med. Coll. of S. C. / Charleston, S C."

276 *Collected Stories of William Faulkner.*

New York: Random House, 1950.
First edition, first printing, with dust jacket.

277 *Collected Stories of William Faulkner.*

New York: Random House, 1950.
First edition, second printing, lacking dust jacket.

Spine stamped in blue and gold. Edges unstained. Correct title on spine.

278 *Collected Stories of William Faulkner.*

New York: Random House, 1950.
First edition, second printing, lacking dust jacket.

Variant binding. Spine stamped in red and gold. Top edge stained light red. Correct title on spine.
Inscribed by Emily Stone on free front endpaper, in blue ink: "Phil and Emily Stone / Oxford / Mississippi."

279 Book-of-the-Month Club brochure announcing *Collected Stories of William Faulkner* as alternate club selection for September 1950.

280 "To the Voters of Oxford."

The "Beer" broadside which Faulkner wrote, had printed, and distributed to the townspeople of Oxford in September 1950. Supports legalized beer sales.

Copy belonged to Malcolm Franklin.

281 "A Name for the City."

Harper's Magazine, 201 (October 1950), 200ff.

First publication of material which became part of *Requiem for a Nun*.

282 *Notes on a Horsethief.*

Greenville, Mississippi: The Levee Press, November 1950.
First edition, only printing, lacking original tissue wrapper.

On spine (as apparently in all copies) "Horse Thief" is two words.
Signed, limited edition of 975 copies. Out-of-series unnumbered copy.
Actual distribution of this book was delayed until January 1951.
Presentation copy given to Phil Stone. On free front endpaper, in Stone's hand, in black ink: "Phil Stone / Oxford, Mississippi / January 29, 1951 / Given to me by Bill at / the office this date when I was / redrawing his will prior to / his leaving for California day / after to-morrow for the / purpose—he says—of doing / a job for Howard Hawks." See item **291**.

283 *Notes on a Horsethief.*

Greenville, Mississippi: The Levee Press, November 1950.
First edition, only printing, with original tissue wrapper.

On spine "Horse Thief" is two words.
Number 590 of signed, limited edition of 975 copies.
Inscribed by Hodding Carter, Kenneth Haxton, and Ben Wasson—the three men responsible for the production of the book.
On half title page, in Carter's hand, in blue ink: "To Louis Brodsky, a Faulkner / collector who should have been / in on the making and especially / the autographing of *Notes on/ a Horse Thief* (neé *A Dangling / Clause from Work in Progress.*) / Hodding Carter."
Beneath that, in Haxton's hand, in black ink: "Hodding got the type, Ben got the / manuscript, I did the supervising. / Regards and best wishes / Kenneth Haxton."
Beneath that, in Wasson's hand, in black ink: "And Bill was more than pleased / with what was accomplished. / Best wishes & keep on collecting, / Ben Wasson."

Laureate, 1945–1962

284 "Faulkner, Bertrand Russell Get Nobel Writing Awards." *The New York Times*, November 11, 1950, pp. 1f.

Accompanied by photograph of Faulkner.
Related article, "Faulkner's Rating by Critics Is High," appears on page 10.

285 "Faulkner Gets '49 Nobel Prize." *New York Herald Tribune*, November 11, 1950, pp. 1f.

Accompanied by photograph of Faulkner on page 5.

286 McMillin, Marguerite. "Nobel Prizewinner William Faulkner: A Gentle Man of Paradoxes." Teletype copy of news feature datelined "Oxford, Miss., Dec 9." "ADVANCE FOR AMS OF SUNDAY, DEC. 10—FROM AP NEWS-FEATURES."

Some of Faulkner's remarks anticipate statements he would make in the Nobel Prize Acceptance Speech in Stockholm, December 10.

287 Photograph of Jill Faulkner in Stockholm, 8¾ by 6¾ inches. By Aftonblade.

Copy belonged to 'Bama McLean.

288 Greeting card from Jill Faulkner to 'Bama McLean. Printed card, made in Sweden, with holograph note.

Text reads:

Dear Aunt Bama,
We had a wonderful time in Stockholm and then went on to Paris and London. Pappy looked so very nice at the presentation ceremony and I was so proud of him and all the ambassadors said what a fine stroke he had made for America in Sweden.
I wont try to tell you how much I appreciated my "mad money" but just say thank you.

Love,
Jill

1951

289 "A Dixie Miss Sees Her Dad Get the Nobel Prize." *The Commercial Appeal*, January 7, 1951, sec. 5, p. 1.

290 "I Decline to Accept the End of Man."

New York Herald Tribune Book Review, January 14, 1951, sec. 6, p. 5.

The Nobel Prize Address.

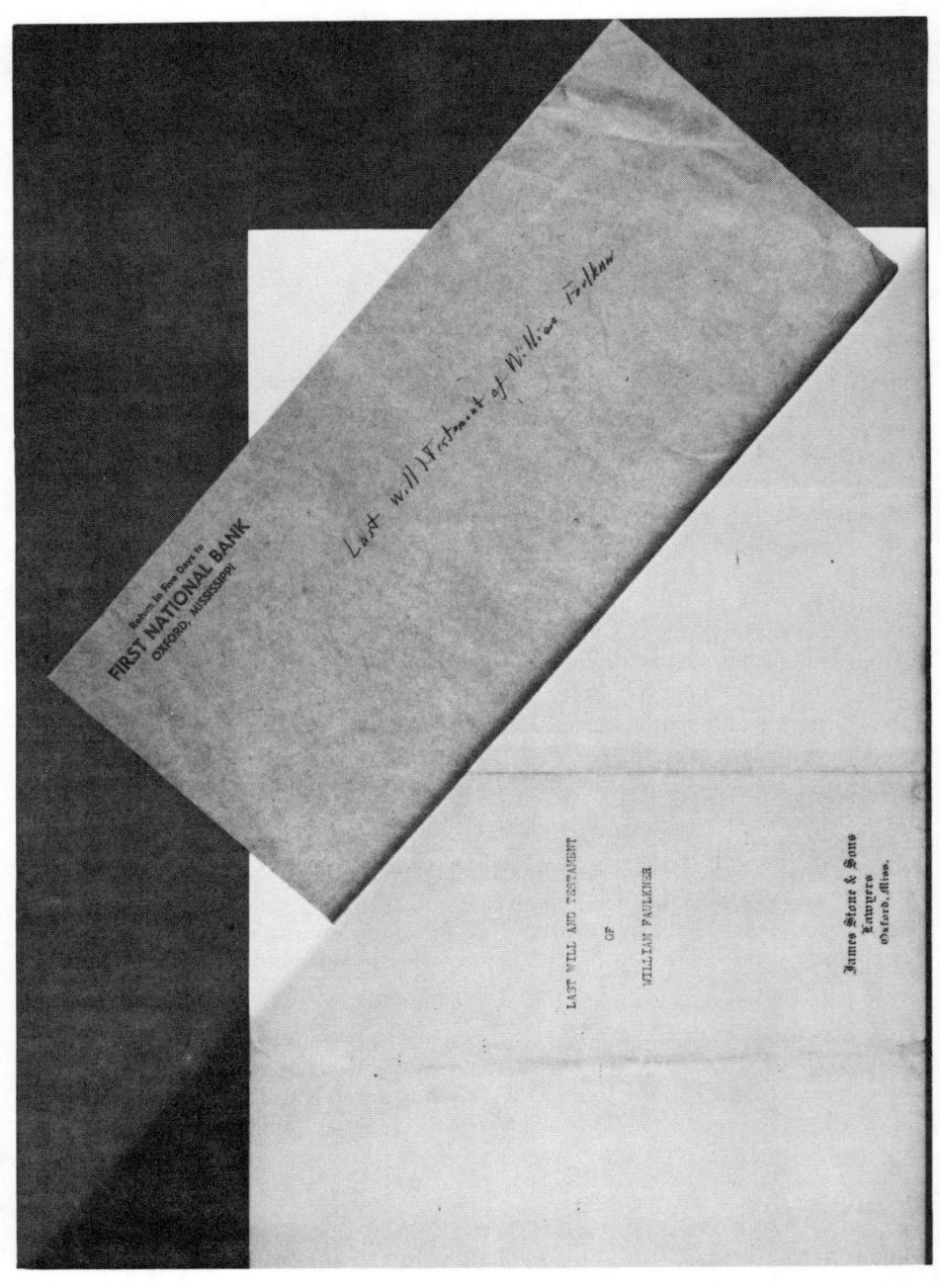

33 Envelope and cover wrapper for Faulkner's 1951 will

long as she shall live. They shall also pay all taxes, insurance and utility bills upon the homestead of my mother and all income taxes on the above monthly payments. These amounts are to be paid out of any part of the income or corpus of my estate and are to take precedence over any legacy or bequest herein made. This Item shall not apply until the insurance left her by item 6 has been exhausted.

ITEM 9.

The above-named Phil Stone and M. C. Falkner and my brother J. W. T. Falkner, III shall each choose one complete manuscript from my manuscripts of they desire. This means a complete manuscript in handscript and any relevant notes and typescript pertaining to such manuscript as may be chosen. Also the above-named M. C. Falkner and J. W. T. Falkner III shall each have from my first editions such volumes as shall give each of them a complete set of my works. After they have made their choice the said Phil Stone shall have from my first editions remaining such volumes as may be necessary to give him a complete set of my works.

ITEM 10.

The residue of my first editions, manuscripts, notes relating thereof, typescripts, etc., are to be held in trust by my Executors and Testamentary Guardians for my daughter, Jill Faulkner, said Executors and Testamentary Guardians being empowered to sell any of such residue when, in their best judgment, such sales are advisable, the revenue from such sales to be used by said Testamentary Guardians for my daughter, Jill Faulkner. In case both of said Testamentary Guardians should die and a successor to them should be appointed by a Court, such successor or successors shall not have the power to sell or publish any part of the above-mentioned material but such material as may remain unsold shall be turned over to some museum or library, or museums or libraries, as may be selected by the Court.

34 Page of Faulkner's 1951 will

291 Last will and testament of William Faulkner, dated February 1, 1951. Signed ribbon typescript, 7 pages, 14 by 8½ inches, unwatermarked. See plates 33 and 34.

All pages except the first and sixth include interlineal changes Faulkner entered in blue ink before signing. Each page signed in blue ink: "1 Feb. 51 / William Faulkner."

With blue stapled wrapper which carries stamp of "James Stone & Sons / Lawyers / Oxford, Miss." and envelope lettered on front in Faulkner's hand, in black ink, "Last Will & Testament of William Faulkner" and signed across seal of back flap, also in black ink, "William Faulkner." Envelope displays return address stamp of First National Bank, Oxford, Mississippi.

See Phil Stone's notation in item **282**.

292 Last will and testament of William Faulkner, dated February 1, 1951. Unsigned carbon typescript of document described in item **291**.

Contains, in Faulkner's hand, in blue-black ink, essentially the same interlineations (with only slight changes in wording) as the ribbon copy.

293 Last will and testament of William Faulkner, dated February 1, 1951. Unsigned carbon typescript of document described in item **291**.

Contains, in Faulkner's hand, in blue-black ink, some but not all of the interlineations on the other copies. Wording also slightly different.

294 "William Falkner, Prize Account," dated February 1, 1951. Signed carbon typescript, 3 pages, 14 by 8½ inches, unwatermarked.

Establishes trust fund of $25,000 from Nobel Prize award. This document is summarized in Blotner, *Faulkner: A Biography*, p. 1374.

295 Nobel Prize Address.

Saturday Review, 34 (February 3, 1951), 4–5.

With a comment by Harrison Smith on page 18.

296 Nobel Prize Address.

The College Omnibus, 7th edition, ed. Leonard F. Dean. New York: Harcourt, Brace, [February] 1951.

Probably the first book appearance. Printed on one leaf (two pages) between preface and part title page. Inserted after table of contents was printed.

297 *The Nobel Prize Speech*.

New York: The Spiral Press, March 1951.

Pamphlet. Gray wrappers printed in red and black. One of initial printing of 1500 copies.

298 *The Nobel Prize Speech.*

New York: The Spiral Press, March 1951.

Reprint of item **297**. One of second printing of 1000 copies.

299 *The Nobel Prize Speech.*

New York: The Spiral Press, March 1951.

Reprint of item **297**. One of third printing of 1000 copies.

300 *William Faulkner on Receiving the Nobel Prize.*

New York: Hunterdon Press, April 1951.

Pamphlet, 3 by 4¼ inches, containing the Nobel Prize Address. One of 200 copies.

301 "The Jail."

Partisan Review, 18 (September–October 1951), 496ff.

First publication of this portion of *Requiem for a Nun*.

302 *Requiem for a Nun.*

New York: Random House, [September 27] 1951.
First edition, first printing, with original acetate jacket. The limited and trade copies of this book are from the same printing.

Number 569 of signed, limited issue of 750 copies.

303 *Requiem for a Nun.*

New York: Random House, 1951.
First edition, first printing, with dust jacket.

Presumably first state of binding. Light green cloth with black spine. Top edge stained dark gray.

Presentation copy given to Phil Stone. On free front endpaper, in blue ink:

Phil, with love. Bill

On title page, in blue ink:

William Faulkner
Oxford, Miss
4 Sept. 1951

On free front endpaper, in Stone's hand, in blue ink: "Phil Stone / Oxford / Mississippi / September 4, 1951."

This book contains Stone's characteristic marginal notations throughout. On blank page facing page 286 Stone has written in black ink:

Well, Bill, this may be a good play (and I know nothing about plays) but if it is I'm entirely wrong. After all, in a play, I would think your audience would have to have some inkling of what the actors are talking about.

As for the prose parts of it are great, — as usual.

I suppose a Faulkner would think he could write a play allright just as he would think he could take God's place and handle the job as well — perhaps a little better than God does.

Oxford, Miss, Oct 6, 1951 (Sunday night.), with Araminta just gone to sleep and Philip writing by the fire.

304 *Requiem for a Nun.*

New York: Random House, 1951.
First edition, first printing, with dust jacket.

Presumably first state of binding.
Presentation copy given to 'Bama McLean. On free front endpaper, in blue ink:

For Aunt Bama
   William Faulkner
   Memphis Tenn
   2 Oct 1951

On title page, in blue ink:

   William Faulkner
   Oxford Miss
   2 October 1951

305 *Requiem for a Nun.*

New York: Random House, 1951.
First edition, first printing, with dust jacket.

Variant binding. Dark green cloth. Top edge unstained. Without flexible cording inside spine strip.

306 *Requiem for a Nun.*

New York: Random House, 1951.
First edition, second printing, with dust jacket.

Binding identical to presumable first state of first printing.

307 *Requiem for a Nun.*

New York: Random House, 1951.
First edition, third printing, with dust jacket.

Binding identical to presumable first state of first printing.

308 *Requiem for a Nun.*

New York: Random House, 1951.
First edition, third printing, lacking dust jacket.

Variant binding. Smooth blue cloth with rough black cloth spine. Gold stamping. Top edge stained black.

309 *Requiem for a Nun.*

London: Chatto & Windus, 1953.
First British edition, first printing, with dust jacket.

310 *Requiem pour une nonne.*

Paris: Gallimard, 1957.
Trans. M. E. Coindreau. Preface by Albert Camus.
First French edition of the novel (Camus' adaptation of the play version published in 1956), with original glassine.

Number 35 of limited issue of 77 copies on "vélin pur fil Lafuma-Navarre."

311 *Requiem for a Nun: A Play from the Novel by William Faulkner.*

New York: Random House, 1959.
Adapted by Ruth Ford.
First edition, first printing, with dust jacket.

Advance review copy, with slip laid in showing publication date as January 30, 1959.

312 Cowley, Malcolm. "In Which Mr. Faulkner Translates Past Into Present." *New York Herald Tribune Book Review*, September 30, 1951, sec. 6, pp. 1f.

Review of *Requiem for a Nun*.
Inscribed by Cowley to Brodsky.

313 Hoffman, Frederick J., and Olga W. Vickery, eds. *William Faulkner: Two Decades of Criticism*. East Lansing: Michigan State College Press, 1951. First edition, first printing, in plain wrappers.

Stitched, unbound advance review copy.
Includes Malcolm Cowley's "Introduction to *The Portable Faulkner*," which is inscribed by Cowley to Brodsky.

314 Hoffman, Frederick J., and Olga W. Vickery, eds. *William Faulkner: Two Decades of Criticism*. East Lansing: Michigan State College Press, 1951. First edition, first printing, with dust jacket.

Includes Malcolm Cowley's "Introduction to *The Portable Faulkner*," which is inscribed "For Louis Brodsky / Malcolm Cowley."

315 *Harvard Advocate*, 135 (November 1951).

"William Faulkner Issue."

Includes "A Note on *Sanctuary*" by Carvel Collins. Inscribed by Collins to Brodsky.

316 *William Faulkner's Speech of Acceptance upon the award of the Nobel Prize for Literature, delivered in Stockholm 10th December, 1950.*

London: Chatto & Windus, December 1951.

Pamphlet.

1952

317 Playbill for premiere performance of *The Fire in the Flint* by M. B. Tolson. Performed by the Dust Bowl Players of Langston University under the auspices of the Oklahoma Conference of the NAACP, June 28, 1952.

Given by Tolson to Faulkner, who in turn gave the item to Malcolm Franklin. Cf. items **330** and **378**.

318 Letter from Phil Stone to Robert Coughlan, dated September 30, 1952, unsigned carbon typescript, 8 pages.

Coughlan had mailed Stone a copy of the manuscript of "The Private World of William Faulkner," the feature Coughlan was preparing for *Life*. In his reply Stone corrected numerous factual errors in the manuscript and made two general suggestions to Coughlan: that he "avoid so much reference to [Faulkner's] drinking" and that he stress "his patience, kindness and tolerance toward young children and old people."

319 "I Decline to Accept the End of Man."

Perspectives U.S.A., No. 1 (Fall 1952), 9–10.

320 Letter from Ward Miner to Phil Stone, dated November 29, 1952, signed ribbon typescript, 1 page.

From Paris. Includes observations about Faulkner's outstanding reputation in France.

321 "Bill Faulkner and the Nobel Prize." Shooting script for the television documentary produced by Ford Foundation and aired on CBS's *Omnibus*, December 1952. Carbon typescript, 10 pages, with penciled corrections made by Phil Stone.

322 "Bill Faulkner and the Nobel Prize." New York: A Transfilm Production, 1952. Print of the *Omnibus* film.

Copy belonged to Phil Stone.

Laureate, 1945–1962

323 Photograph of Faulkner and Phil Stone. Glossy print, 5 by 7 inches.

View of Faulkner and Stone in Stone's law office during the filming of Ford Foundation documentary for CBS's *Omnibus* program.
Stamped on verso: "Portrait by 'Col.' Cofield."
This photograph reproduced in Blotner, *Faulkner: A Biography*, p. 1438.

324 Aldridge, John W., ed. *Critiques and Essays on Modern Fiction 1920–1951*. New York: The Ronald Press, 1952.

Copy belonged to Malcolm Cowley. Inscribed by Cowley to Brodsky.
Includes "An Introduction to William Faulkner" by Cowley. First printing in complete form of this essay, portions of which had previously appeared as "Introduction" to *The Portable Faulkner* and "William Faulkner's Legend of the South," *Sewanee Review*, 53 (Summer 1945), 343–361.

325 Miner, Ward L. *The World of William Faulkner*. Durham, North Carolina: Duke University Press, [1952]. Printed in France.

1 9 5 3

326 Codicil to Faulkner's 1951 will, dated January 26, 1953. Unsigned carbon typescript, 2 pages, 14 by 8½ inches, watermarked "TROJAN ONION SKIN / EAGLE-A."

Names Saxe Commins as Faulkner's literary executor.

327 Coughlan, Robert. "The Private World of William Faulkner." *Life*, 35 (September 28, 1953), 118–136.

328 *Mirrors of Chartres Street*.

Minneapolis: Faulkner Studies, [November 30] 1953.
First edition, only printing, with dust jacket.

Number 283 in limited edition of 1000 copies.
Reprints eleven prose sketches Faulkner published in the New Orleans *Times-Picayune* in 1925.

329 *Mirrors of Chartres Street*.

Minneapolis: Faulkner Studies, 1953.
First edition, only printing, without dust jacket, as issued.

Variant binding. Gray cloth stamped on spine in black and red.
Certificate of limitation page is unnumbered, with the following holograph notation, in black ink: "This is no. 2 / of thirteen copies of a / press overrun / bound by Allan Campbell, / Minneapolis, Sept. 1957."

1954

330 *Liberia today*, 3 (February 1954).

Publication of Liberian Embassy in Washington. This issue features M. B. Tolson, a black playwright and poet, author of "Libretto for the Republic of Liberia."

Inscribed on page 3, in blue ink, beside a picture of Tolson being toasted by the Liberian ambassador: "To William Faulkner / from / M. B. Tolson."

Faulkner subsequently gave this magazine to Malcolm Franklin. See also items **317** and **378**.

331 *The Faulkner Reader: Selections from the Works of William Faulkner.*

New York: Random House, [April 1] 1954.
First edition, first printing, with dust jacket.

Book-of-the-Month Club edition with "W" on copyright page.
First appearance of Faulkner's "Foreword," plus reprints of *The Sound and the Fury*, "Old Man," several stories and excerpts, and the Nobel Prize address.

332 *The Faulkner Reader: Selections from the Works of William Faulkner.*

New York: The Modern Library, 1959.
First edition, reprint, with dust jacket.

"First Modern Library Giant Edition" (G82).

333 "Notes on a Horse Thief."

Vogue, 124 (July 1954), 46ff.

Story which was incorporated into *A Fable*.

334 Cowley, Malcolm. "Faulkner's Powerful New Novel: Biblical Overtones, Daring Symbols." *New York Herald Tribune Book Review*, August 1, 1954, sec. 6, pp. 1f.

Review of *A Fable*. Inscribed on page 1, in black ink: "For Louis Brodsky, happily inscribed, Malcolm Cowley—12/12/78."

335 *A Fable*.

New York: Random House, [August 2] 1954.
First edition, first printing, with original glassine, boxed. The limited and trade copies of this book are from the same printing.

Number 479 of signed, limited issue of 1000 copies.

336 *A Fable*.

New York: Random House, 1954.
First edition, first printing, with dust jacket.

Presentation copy given to Phil Stone. On free front endpaper, in black ink:

Laureate, 1945–1962

Phil, with love
                    Bill
Oxford, Miss
10 June 1954

On title page, in black ink:

William Faulkner
10 June 1954

On both free front endpaper and half title page, in Stone's hand, in black ink: "Phil Stone / Oxford, Mississippi / June 10, 1954."

337 A *Fable*.

New York: Random House, 1954.
First edition, first printing, with dust jacket.

Tipped in between front paste-down and free front endpaper is portion of legal document dated "August 3, 1948" and signed, in blue ink, "William Faulkner."

This fragment bears similarities to the movie contracts which Faulkner signed with Loew's Incorporated (MGM). It may be a part of Faulkner's first contract for the sale of *Intruder in the Dust* to MGM. As Blotner points out (*Faulkner: A Biography*, p. 1260), Faulkner and his notary had made errors in the original document and a second one had to be executed on August 16. Apparently someone who prized Faulkner's signature in any form clipped the signed part of the voided document and tipped it into this copy of *A Fable*.

338 A *Fable*.

New York: Random House, 1954.
First edition, first printing, with dust jacket.

339 A *Fable*.

London: Chatto & Windus, 1955.
First British edition, first printing, with dust jacket.

Enclosed in yellow band which reads: "Awarded the / Pulitzer Prize for Literature / Book Society Recommendation."

340 *Parabole*.

Paris: Gallimard, 1958.
Trans. R. N. Raimbault.
First French edition, lacking original glassine.

Number 25 of limited issue of 76 copies on "vélin pur fil Lafuma-Navarre."

341 Last will and testament of William Faulkner, dated "August __, 1954." Unsigned carbon typescript, 6 pages, 14 by 8½ inches, watermarked "TROJAN ONION SKIN / EAGLE-A."

With blue cover wrapper which carries typed title, "LAST WILL AND TESTAMENT / OF / WILLIAM FAULKNER / (COPY)" and stamp of "James Stone & Sons / Lawyers / Oxford, Miss."

342 Last will and testament of William Faulkner, dated "August __, 1954." Duplicate of item **341**, without blue cover wrapper.

343 Collins, Carvel. *The Interior Monologues of The Sound and the Fury*. *Publications in the Humanities* (Department of Humanities, Massachusetts Institution of Technology), No. 6 [1954].

Monograph. Reprints essay from *English Institute Essays 1952*, ed. Alan S. Downer (New York: Columbia University Press, 1954), pp. 29–56.

Copy belonged to Collins. Inscribed by Collins to Brodsky, on title page, in black ink: "For L. D., / This first reprinting—I think—of an essay in / *English Institute Essays*, 1952 / —Carvel."

344 Letter from Phil Stone to Carvel Collins, dated August 16, 1954, unsigned carbon typescript, 5 pages.

Discusses the genesis of *The Sound and the Fury*. In response to Collins' monograph entitled *The Interior Monologues of The Sound and the Fury*, which Stone had read the night before.

345 Letter from Phil Stone to Robert Coughlan, dated October 6, 1954, unsigned carbon typescript, 1 page.

Includes the following observation:

One of the best things about Bill's writing is the deliberate withholding of information. This creates suspense and also makes the reader feel that he is sharing himself in working out the solution. This is more or less the same method that is used in detective stories and is absolutely sound.

346 *São Paulo: Fastest Growing City in the World*. Amsterdam: Livraria Kosmos Editora, 1954. First edition, first printing, with dust jacket. Unnumbered copy of deluxe limited edition of 350 copies.

This pictorial geography was given to Faulkner in honor of his participation in the celebration of the quadricentennial of the city of São Paulo. Inscribed on title page: "To William Faulkner / from your Brazilian / friend / Osmar Pimentel. / S Paulo, / 10/8/54."

Faulkner subsequently gave the book to Malcolm Franklin.

347 "Notes on a Horse Thief."

Perspectives U.S.A., No. 9 (Autumn 1954), 24–59.

From *A Fable*.

348 *Faulkner Studies*, 3 (Winter 1954).

First reprint of two prose sketches, "Jealousy" (46–50) and "Episode" (51–53), which Faulkner wrote in 1925 for the New Orleans *Times-Picayune*.
Later collected in *New Orleans Sketches*.

349 Coughlan, Robert. "The Private World of William Faulkner." *Prize Articles 1954*, ed. Llewellyn Miller. New York: Ballantine Books, 1954, pp. 121–156. First edition, first printing, with dust jacket.

Reprints the articles from September 28, 1953, and October 5, 1953, issues of *Life*.

350 Coughlan, Robert. *The Private World of William Faulkner*. New York: Harper & Brothers, Publishers, 1954. First edition, first printing, with dust jacket.

Expands the 1953 *Life* articles.

351 Coughlan, Robert. *The Private World of William Faulkner*. New York: Avon Books, [ca. 1962].

Avon paperback G-1144.

352 *Literature in the Modern World: Lectures Delivered at George Peabody College for Teachers 1951–1954*. Nashville, Tennessee: George Peabody College for Teachers, 1954.

Includes "Faulkner's Reputation and the Contemporary Novel" by Carvel Collins.
Copy belonged to Collins. Inscribed on title page, in black ink: "For L. D., this / Faulknerian / drumming from an / earlier campaign. / —Carvel."

353 Cowley, Malcolm. *The Literary Situation*. New York: The Viking Press, 1954. Compass Books Edition, second printing, December 1960.

Includes numerous references to Faulkner.
Inscribed by Cowley to Brodsky.

1955

354 Quitclaim deed executed by Jill Faulkner Summers, dated "March __, 1955." Unsigned carbon typescript, 2 pages, 14 by 8½ inches, watermarked "Neenah Onionskin."

Conveys life estate in Rowan Oak to William and Estelle Oldham Faulkner. Corrects inadvertent error in deed of June 24, 1954.

355 *New Orleans Sketches*.

Tokyo: Hokuseido Press, [April 1] 1955.

Ed. Ichiro Nishizaki.
First edition, first printing, with dust jacket.

   Dark blue cloth.
   Reprints thirteen of the prose sketches Faulkner wrote in 1925 for the New Orleans *Times-Picayune*: the eleven collected in *Mirrors of Chartres Street*, plus "Jealousy" and "Episode."

356 *New Orleans Sketches*.

Tokyo: Hokuseido Press, 1955.
Ed. Ichiro Nishizaki.
First edition, first printing, with dust jacket.

   Medium blue cloth.

357 *New Orleans Sketches*.

Tokyo: Hokuseido Press, 1955.
Ed. Ichiro Nishizaki.
First edition, first printing, in tan mottled wrappers.

358 *New Orleans Sketches*.

New Brunswick: Rutgers University Press, 1958.
Ed. with introduction by Carvel Collins.
First American edition, first printing, with dust jacket.

   Inscribed by Collins to Brodsky.
   Reprints all sixteen of the 1925 *Times-Picayune* sketches, as well as "New Orleans" from *The Double Dealer*, 7 (January–February 1925), 102–107.

359 *New Orleans Sketches*.

New York: Grove Press, 1961.
Ed. with introduction by Carvel Collins.
First American edition, reprint, in paperback.

   First Evergreen edition (E-292).
   Inscribed on half title page, in black ink: "For Hubert Starr / —Carvel Collins."

360 *New Orleans Sketches*.

New York: Grove Press, 1961.
Ed. with introduction by Carvel Collins.
First American edition, reprint, in paperback.

   First Evergreen edition (E-292).
   Inscribed by Collins to Brodsky.

361 *New Orleans Sketches*.

New York: Random House, 1968.

Ed. with introduction by Carvel Collins.
Second American edition, first printing, with dust jacket.

> Copy belonged to Collins. Inscribed by Collins to Brodsky.

362 *New Orleans Sketches.*

New York: Random House, 1968.
Ed. with introduction by Carvel Collins.
Second American edition, third printing, with dust jacket.

> Inscribed by Collins to Brodsky.

363 *New Orleans Sketches.*

London: Sidgwick and Jackson Limited, 1959.
Ed. with introduction by Carvel Collins.
First American edition, first British reprint, lacking dust jacket.

> Black boards.
> Copy belonged to Collins. Inscribed by Collins, on title page, in black ink: "For L. D. Brodsky / —Carvel."

364 *New Orleans Sketches.*

London: Sidgwick and Jackson Limited, 1959.
Ed. with introduction by Carvel Collins.
First American edition, first British reprint, with dust jacket.

> Dark blue boards. Has blue tape over copyright notification.
> Inscribed by Collins to Brodsky.

365 *New Orleans Sketches.*

London: Brown, Watson Ltd., 1958.
Ed. with introduction by Carvel Collins.
First American edition, second British reprint (after 1960), in paperback.

> Digit paperback (R442).
> Inscribed by Collins to Brodsky.

366 *Historias de Nueva Orleans.*

Barcelona: Luis de Caralt, 1964.
Ed. with introduction by Carvel Collins.
First Spanish edition, first printing, with dust jacket.

> Copy belonged to Collins. Inscribed on page 31, in black ink: "For L. D. Brodsky, / who probably / can read this. / I can't / —Carvel."

367 "On Privacy: The American Dream: What Happened to It."

Harper's Magazine, 211 (July 1955), 33–38.

> Essay by Faulkner. See item **273**.

368 Mohrt, Michel. *Le nouveau romain americain*. Paris: Gallimard, 1955.
First edition, first printing, with original glassine.

Unnumbered S.P. copy. Inscribed by author to the publisher. On half title page, in blue ink: "A Pierre Gallimard, / Amical hommage de / M Mohrt."
Laid in is prospectus showing date of publication as May 1955.
Contains two pieces on Faulkner: "William Faulkner: ou une religion du temps" and "Note: A *Fable*, 'Nouveau Testament' de Faulkner."

369 *Jealousy and Episode: Two Stories by William Faulkner*.

Minneapolis: Faulkner Studies, [September 1]1955.

Number 190 of limited edition of 500 copies.
Two prose sketches from 1925 New Orleans *Times-Picayune*.

370 *Big Woods*.

Page proof, tied in brown manila wrappers. 7 pages of prelims, plus text numbering 3–212. Printed on white label on wrapper: "Uncorrected proof from / Random House / BIG WOODS / by / William Faulkner / for ADVANCE readers."

Copy belonged to Malcolm Cowley. Inscribed on half title page, in blue ink: "This set of galleys was the / one ['for' *del.*] from which I reviewed / *The Big Woods*. It is notable / for the / different-/from-before versions of *The Bear* / (without Part IV) and *Delta Autumn*. / Malcolm Cowley."
Contains Cowley's annotations, in pencil, throughout.

371 *Big Woods*.

New York: Random House, [October 14] 1955.
First edition, first printing, with dust jacket.

Presentation copy. On free front endpaper, in blue-black ink:

> *Phil Stone, with love*
> *Bill*

On title page, in blue-black ink:

> *William Faulkner*
> *Oxford, Miss*
> *3 Nov. 1955*

Big Woods contains four previously-published stories ("The Bear," "The Old People," "A Bear Hunt," and "Race at Morning"), plus linking interchapters and an epilogue.

372 *Big Woods*.

New York: Random House, 1955.
First edition, first printing, with dust jacket.

Presentation copy given to 'Bama McLean. On free front endpaper, in blue-black ink:

Laureate, 1945–1962

To Aunt Bama, with love
William Faulkner

On title page, in blue-black ink:

William Faulkner
New York
13 Nov. 1955

373 *Big Woods.*

New York: Random House, 1955.
First edition, first printing, with dust jacket.

Front flap of jacket shows $3.95 price and date "10/55." Back of jacket carries advertisement for A *Fable*.

374 *Big Woods.*

New York: Random House, 1955.
First edition, second printing, with dust jacket.

Front flap of jacket shows $3.95 price but no date. Back of jacket lists thirteen Random House titles by Faulkner.

375 *Big Woods.*

New York: Random House, 1955.
First edition, fourth printing, with dust jacket.

Cloth and top edge of this copy slightly darker green than those of first and second printings.
Front flap of jacket shows price of $4.95. Back of jacket lists twenty-two Random House titles by Faulkner, including *The Wishing Tree* (published April 11, 1967).

376 Peyre, Henri. *The Contemporary French Novel.* New York: Oxford University Press, 1955. First edition, third printing (1959), with dust jacket.

Contains numerous references to Faulkner.
Inscribed by Peyre to Brodsky.

1 9 5 6

377 *Three Views of the Segregation Decision.* Southern Regional Council, Atlanta, Georgia, 1956.

Pamphlet which reproduces papers read by Faulkner, Benjamin E. Mays, and Cecil Sims at meeting of Southern Historical Association, Memphis, Tennessee, November 10, 1955. Foreword by Bell I. Wiley.
Includes "American Segregation and the World Crisis" by Faulkner.

378 Tolson, Melvin B. *Rendezvous with America*. New York: Dodd, Mead & Company, 1944.

   Presentation copy given to Faulkner, who in turn gave the book to Malcolm Franklin.
   Inscribed by Tolson to Faulkner. On free front endpaper: "To William Faulkner— / A rock in a weary land— / M. B. Tolson / Langston University, / Langston City, / Oklahoma, / April 17, 1956."
   Tolson, a black poet and playwright, had been impressed with Faulkner's strong anti-segregation stand and his statements concerning the murder of Emmett Till, a young black, by two white Mississippians. See items **317** and **330**.

379 *Jefferson, Mississippi*.

Paris: Le Club du meilleur livre, 1956. Ed. with introduction by Michel Mohrt.
First edition, with original acetate dust jacket.

   Number 2601 of limited edition of 5500 copies.
   Contains representative selections from Faulkner's published work.

1957

380 Letter from Phil Stone to James Meriwether, dated February 19, 1957, unsigned carbon typescript, 4 pages.

   Discusses the upcoming Princeton University exhibit of Faulkner materials, with additional comments on the history of Faulkner's Snopes saga and Faulkner's relationship to the French Symbolist poets.

381 Letter from William S. Dix to Phil Stone, dated April 24, 1957, ribbon typescript, 1 page.

   Acknowledges receipt of Stone's copies of the typescripts of *The Hamlet* and *The Wishing Tree* for display during the Princeton exhibit of Faulkner materials.
   Accompanied by brochure announcing the annual meeting of the Friends of Princeton Library, which formally opened the exhibit on May 10.

382 *The Town*.

New York: Random House, [May 1] 1957.
First edition, first printing, with acetate dust jacket. The limited and trade copies of this book are from the same printing.

   Number 300 of signed, limited issue of 450 copies.

383 *The Town*.

New York: Random House, 1957.
First edition, first printing, with dust jacket.

   Presumably first state of binding. Wine red cloth stamped in gold and gray. Top edge stained blue-gray. Threaded gray endpapers.

Front flap of jacket carries date "5/57."
Dedication page reads: "To Phil Stone / He did half the laughing for thirty years" (see plate 38).
Presentation copy given to Stone. On half title page, in blue-black ink (see plate 36):

> *To Phil Stone*
> *With Love*
> *William Faulkner*

On title page, in blue-black ink:

> *William Faulkner*

On free front endpaper, in Stone's hand, in blue ball point: "Phil Stone / Oxford, Mississippi / April 1957."

384 *The Town.*

New York: Random House, 1957.
First edition, first printing, with dust jacket.

Presumably first state of binding. Front flap of jacket carries date "5/57."
Presentation copy. On free front endpaper, in black ink:

> *M. A. Franklin*
> *To Buddy, with love*
> *Pappy*

On title page, in black ink:

> *William Faulkner*
> *Charlottesville, Va*
> *4 May 1957*

On trilogy title page, in Franklin's hand, in blue ball point: "Malcolm A. Franklin / Oxford, Mississippi (??) / 4 May 1957."

385 *The Town.*

New York: Random House, 1957.
First edition, first printing, with dust jacket.

Presumably first state of binding. Front flap of jacket carries date "5/57."

386 *The Town.*

New York: Random House, 1957.
First edition, first printing, with dust jacket.

Presumably first state of binding. Front flap of jacket carries no date.

387 *The Town.*

New York: Random House, 1957.
First edition, first printing, with dust jacket.

Variant binding. Gray beige cloth stamped in black and green. Top edge unstained. Threaded gray endpapers.
Front flap of jacket carries date "5/57."

388 *The Town.*

New York: Random House, 1957.
First edition, first printing, with dust jacket.

Variant binding. Orange cloth stamped in black and green. Top edge stained green. Plain endpapers.
Front flap of jacket carries no date.

389 *The Town.*

New York: Random House, 1957.
First edition, first printing, with dust jacket.

Variant binding. Orange cloth stamped in black and green. Top edge stained green. Plain endpapers.
On spine of this copy the "T" in "Town" is broken.
Front flap of jacket carries no date.

390 *The Town.*

New York: Random House, 1957.
First edition, second printing, with dust jacket.

Wine red cloth stamped in gold and gray. Top edge stained dark blue. Threaded gray endpapers.
Front flap of jacket carries no date.

391 *The Town.*

London: Chatto and Windus, 1958.
First British edition, first printing, with dust jacket.

392 *La ville.*

Paris: Gallimard, 1962.
Trans. J. and L. Breant.
First French edition, with original glassine.

Number 11 of limited issue of 66 copies on "vélin pur fil Lafuma-Navarre."

393 "The Waifs."

The Saturday Evening Post, 229 (May 4, 1957), 26ff.

Excerpt from *The Town*.

394 "The Literary Career of William Faulkner: An Exhibition." Souvenir leaflet of the Princeton University exhibit of Faulkner materials, May 10–August 30, 1957.

Laureate, 1945–1962

Inscribed on front cover, "For James Bloom," and on last page, "Jim Meriwether."

395 *The Princeton University Library Chronicle*, 18 (Spring 1957).

A Faulkner issue published in conjunction with the Faulkner exhibit at Princeton University Library. Includes "William Faulkner: A Check List" by James Meriwether. Inscribed by Meriwether to James Bloom.

396 Meriwether, James B. *William Faulkner: A Check List*. Princeton, New Jersey: Princeton University Library, 1957.

Reprinted from *The Princeton University Library Chronicle*, 18 (Spring 1957), 136–158.
In green wrappers. Inscribed by Meriwether to Brodsky.

1 9 5 8

397 Letter from Phil Stone to Maud Falkner, dated February 14, 1958, unsigned carbon typescript, 1 page.

This letter to Faulkner's mother, in agreement with a note she had sent Stone, criticizes the NAACP and opposes federally-enforced integration.

398 *The University of Virginia Magazine*, 2 (Spring 1958).

Includes two Faulkner items: "A Word to Virginians" (11–14) and "William Faulkner On Dialect" (32–38). Edited by Joseph Blotner. Both of these items appear in *Faulkner in the University*, though the second is considerably condensed.
Inscribed on front cover, in black ink: "For L. D. Brodsky, / twenty years later, / with best wishes, / Joseph Blotner / 6 Dec 1978."

399 Correspondence between Harold Ober Associates and Phil Stone regarding codicil to Faulkner's will concerning movie rights to *The Hamlet*.

a. Ober to Stone, March 11, 1958, signed ribbon typescript, 2 pages. Enclosed with letter was two-page typescript of codicil recommended by Twentieth Century-Fox.

b. Stone to Harold Ober Associates, March 14, 1958, unsigned carbon typescript, 1 page.

c. Anne Louise Davis to Stone, May 13, 1958, signed ribbon typescript, 1 page.

d. Stone to Anne Louise Davis, May 15, 1958, unsigned carbon typescript, 1 page.

e. Stone to Ober, October 10, 1958, unsigned carbon typescript, 1 page.

f. Ober to Stone, October 15, 1958, signed ribbon typescript, 1 page.

The six-month delay in Faulkner's signing of the codicil (see item **400**) was caused, according to Stone, by Faulkner's procrastination.

400   Codicil to Faulkner's will, dated October 10, 1958. Signed carbon typescript, 3 pages, 14 by 8½ inches, watermarked "MANIFOLD / NEKOOSA / MADE IN U.S.A."

Typescript date of "March __, 1958," is revised in blue ink to "October 10, 1958" (see item **399**).
Each page is signed "William Faulkner."
With blue stapled wrapper on which is typed: "CODICIL / TO / WILL OF WILLIAM FAULKNER." Wrapper carries stamp of "James Stone & Sons / Lawyers / Box 269 / Oxford, Miss."
This document pertains to April 1, 1957, agreement with Twentieth Century-Fox Corporation concerning movie rights to *The Hamlet*.

401   Codicil to Faulkner's will, dated "March __, 1958." Unsigned carbon typescript, 3 pages. Copy of document described in item **400**. Without wrapper.

402   Codicil to Faulkner's will, dated "March __, 1958." Unsigned carbon typescript, 3 pages. Another copy of document described in item **400**. Without wrapper.

403   "20th Century Fox Exhibitor's Campaign Manual," 12 pages. Illustrates promotional material for *The Long, Hot Summer*, the movie version of *The Hamlet*.

404   *The University of Virginia Magazine*, 2 (Winter 1958).

Includes "William Faulkner On Dialect" (7–13), the first of two radio interviews with Faulkner circulated by the Department of Speech and Drama of the University of Virginia. Edited by Joseph Blotner.
Inscribed by Blotner to Brodsky.

405   *Three Famous Short Novels*.

New York: Random House, 1958.
Modern Library paperback (P36).

Contains "Spotted Horses," "Old Man," and "The Bear."

406   *Three Famous Short Novels*.

New York: Vintage Books, 1958.
Vintage paperback (V-149).

407   Herlihy, James Leo, and William Noble. *Blue Denim*. New York: Random House, 1958. First edition, first printing, with dust jacket.

A play from William Faulkner's library. Given by Faulkner to Malcolm Franklin. This title does not appear in Blotner, comp., *William Faulkner's Library*.

1959

408 Stone, Philip Alston. *No Place to Run*. New York: The Viking Press, 1959. First edition, first printing, with dust jacket.

Novel by Phil Stone's son, Faulkner's godson (see items **208** and **264**).
Presentation copy given to Myrtle Ramey Demarest. Inscribed on title page, in black ink: "Philip Alston Stone."
Accompanied by typescript letter, 1 page, dated April 27, 1959, from "Philip" to "Miss Lynda" (Mrs. Demarest's sister), noting that copy of novel had been sent to Mrs. Demarest.

409 "William Faulkner: Man Working 1919–1959." Souvenir pamphlet of exhibit mounted at Alderman Library, University of Virginia, October 1–December 23, 1959.

Reproduces page 1 from corrected typescript used for setting copy of *The Mansion*.

410 *William Faulkner: An Exhibition of Manuscripts*. Catalogue to accompany the Faulkner exhibit at the Research Center, The University of Texas at Austin, beginning October 15, 1959. Exhibit arranged and coordinated by James Meriwether.

Number 301 of limited edition of 500 copies.
Inscribed by Meriwether to James Bloom.

411 *William Faulkner: An Exhibition of Manuscripts*. Catalogue to accompany the Faulkner exhibit at the Research Center, The University of Texas at Austin, beginning October 15, 1959.

Number 400 of limited edition of 500 copies.
Copy belonged to Phil Stone.

412 *William Faulkner: An Exhibition of Manuscripts*. Catalogue to accompany the Faulkner exhibit at the Research Center, The University of Texas at Austin, beginning October 15, 1959.

Number 299 of limited edition of 500 copies.
Inscribed by James Meriwether, the coordinator of the exhibit, to Brodsky.

413 *The Mansion*.

Temporarily paged galley proof. Galleys 1–153 with prelims added. Section pages VI and VII are reversed. Blue paper covers with blue plastic spiral binding.

Printed cover reads: "Uncorrected Proof from / RANDOM HOUSE / THE MANSION / by William Faulkner."
Written in unidentified hand in blue ball point on cover: "Publ. date–Oct. 29 / $4.75."

35 Faulkner's inscription to Phil Stone in *The Hamlet*

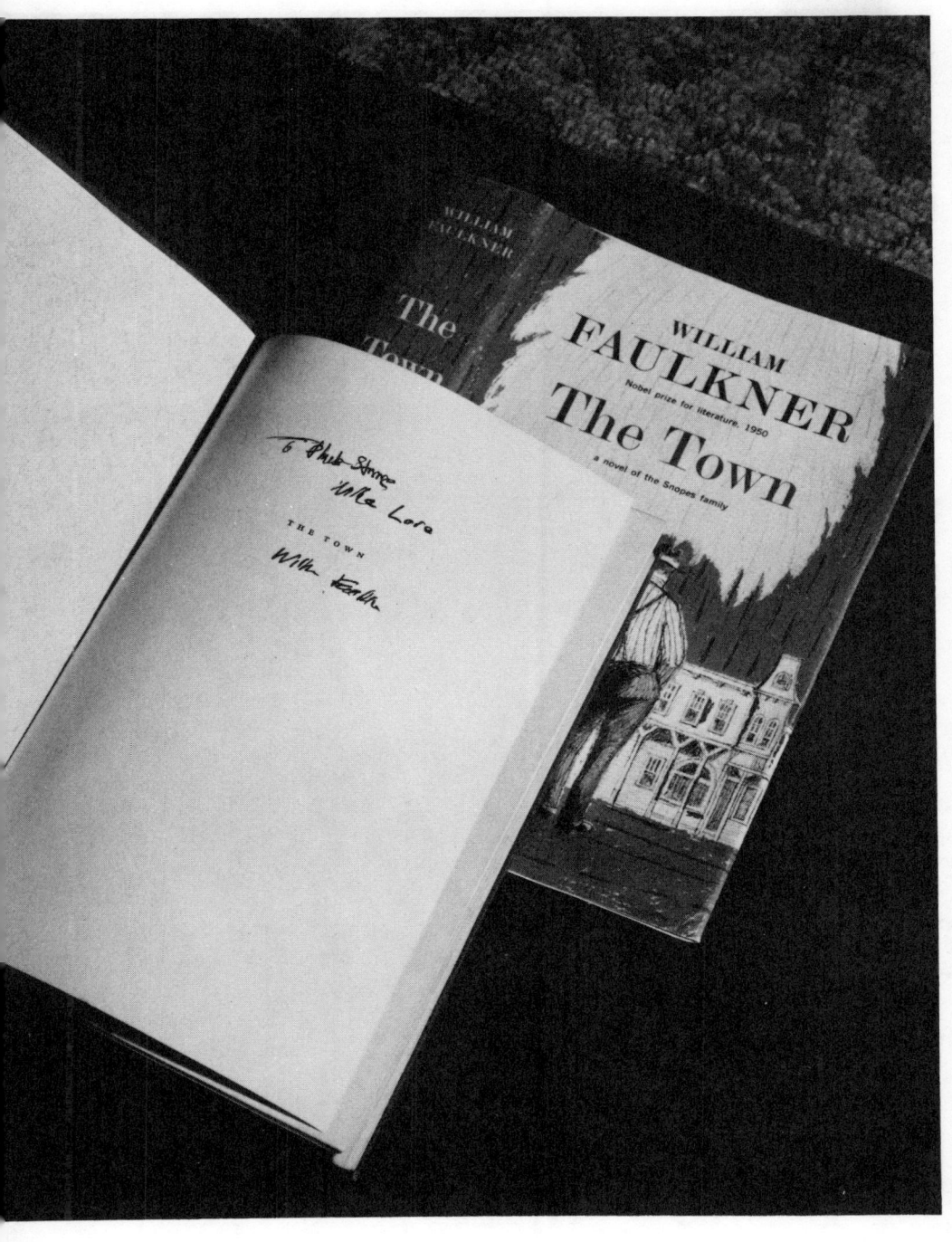

36 Faulkner's inscription to Phil Stone in *The Town*

37　Faulkner's inscription to Phil Stone in *The Mansion*

38 Dedication page of *The Town*

Inscribed, in black ink, on front cover, "Malcolm Cowley," and on page II, "For Louis Brodsky: / These bound galleys are what / I read before reviewing *The Mansion* / for the New York Times Book / Review (issue of Nov. 15, 1959, pp. / 1 and 18). / Malcolm Cowley."

414   *The Mansion*.

New York: Random House, [November 13] 1959.
First edition, first printing, with original tissue. The limited and trade copies of this book are from the same printing.

Number 303 of signed, limited issue of 500 copies.

415   *The Mansion*.

New York: Random House, 1959.
First edition, first printing, with dust jacket.

Dedication page reads: "To Phil Stone."
Presentation copy given to Stone. On free front endpaper, in blue ink (see plate 37):

*To Phil Stone
from Bill*

On title page, in blue ink:

*William Faulkner
Oxford, Miss
5 Oct. 1959*

On free front endpaper, in Stone's hand, in blue ball point: "Phil Stone / Oxford, Mississippi / October 9, 1959."

416   *The Mansion*.

New York: Random House, 1959.
First edition, first printing, with dust jacket.

Presentation copy given to Malcolm Franklin. On free front endpaper, in blue ink:

*To Buddy, with love
Pappy*

On title page, in blue ink:

*William Faulkner
3 Dec 1960*

On front paste-down, in Franklin's hand, in pencil: "M A Franklin / 46 Queen St. / CharlesTown / S.C."

417   *The Mansion*.

New York: Random House, 1959.
First edition, first printing, with dust jacket.

418 *The Mansion.*

New York: Random House, 1959.
First edition, second printing, with dust jacket.

419 *The Mansion.*

London: Chatto and Windus, 1961.
First British edition, first printing, with dust jacket.

420 *Le domaine.*

Paris: Gallimard, 1962.
Trans. René Hilleret.
First French edition, with original glassine.

Number 45 of limited issue of 66 copies on "vélin pur fil Lafuma-Navarre."

421 Collins, Carvel. "Foreword" to Signet Classics edition of *The Unvanquished*. Carbon typescript, 8 pages.

Accompanied by cover letter from Collins to 'Bama McLean, dated November 6, 1959, signed ribbon typescript, 1 page.
Collins mailed Mrs. McLean the carbon of the foreword in appreciation for the assistance she had provided in Collins' research.

422 Cowley, Malcolm. "Flem Snopes Gets His Come-Uppance." *The New York Times Book Review*, November 15, 1959, pp. 1f.

Review of *The Mansion*. See item **413**.
Inscribed by Cowley to Brodsky.

423 "Mink Snopes."

Esquire, 52 (December 1959), 226ff.

Excerpt from *The Mansion*.

424 Gwynn, Frederick L., and Joseph L. Blotner, eds. *Faulkner in the University: Class Conferences at the University of Virginia 1957–1958*. Charlottesville: University of Virginia Press, 1959. First edition, first printing, with dust jacket.

Notice of publication laid in.
Inscribed on free front endpaper, in blue ink: "With thanks for a very / pleasant evening / April 23, 1963   C Waller Barrett."
Also on free front endpaper, in black ink: "With best regards and / pleasure at this further / association with my old / and admired friend, Waller Barrett, / for L. D. Brodsky— / Joseph Blotner."
Inscribed on title page, in black ink: "Joseph Blotner / 6 Dec 1978."

425 Gwynn, Frederick L., and Joseph L. Blotner, eds. *Faulkner in the Uni-*

versity: Class Conferences at the University of Virginia 1957–1958. New York: Vintage Books, 1965. First Vintage edition.

Vintage paperback (V-269).
Inscribed by Blotner to Brodsky.

426 Gwynn, Frederick L., and Joseph L. Blotner, eds. *Gespräche mit Faulkner*. Stuttgart: Henry Goverts Verlag, 1961. First German edition, in wrappers.

Inscribed by Blotner to Brodsky.

427 Gwinn [sic], Frederick L., and Joseph L. Blotner, eds. *Faulkner à l'Université: cours et conférences prononcés a l'université de Virginie (1957–1958) par William Faulkner*. Paris: Gallimard, 1964. Trans. René Hilleret. Introduction by J. Gresset. First French edition, with original glassine.

Number 10 of 49 copies on "vélin pur fil Lafuma-Navarre."
Inscribed on free front endpaper, in black ink: "For L. D. Brodsky, / with best French / greetings in Anglais— / Joseph Blotner." On title page, in black ink: "Joseph Blotner / 6 Dec 1978."

428 Sewall, Richard B. *The Vision of Tragedy*. New Haven: Yale University Press, 1959. First edition, third printing (November 1960), with dust jacket.

Contains, on pages 133–147, "*Absalom, Absalom!*"
Inscribed by author on free front endpaper, in blue ink: "To Louis Brodsky— / Faulknerian extraordinaire / [rule] / Richard B. Sewall / Feb. 1963."

429 Giannitrapani, Angela Minissi. *La New Orleans e la Louisiana del Faulkner*. Napoli, 1959.

Monograph mailed by the author to Phil Stone. Card stapled inside front cover contains inscription to Stone and Faulkner. Stone has signed the booklet on cover and on page 265.

430 Giannitrapani, Angela. "Wistaria: Le Immagini in Faulkner." *Studi Americani 5*, Roma, 1959.

Mailed by the author to Phil Stone. Inscribed by Stone on inside of front cover, in black ink: "Phil Stone / Oxford, Miss / July 7, 1960 / Philip's 20th birthday."

1 9 6 0

431 Meriwether, James B. "The Literary Career of William Faulkner: Catalogue of an Exhibition in the Princeton University Library," *The Princeton University Library Chronicle*, 21 (Spring 1960), 111–164.

Inscribed on page 111, in blue ink: "For Louis D. Brodsky / with the compliments of / James B Meriwether."

432 *Northwestern Library News*, 14 (May 13, 1960). Contains announcement of exhibit of Carl Petersen's Faulkner collection, Deering Library, Northwestern University, Evanston, Illinois, Spring 1960.

Inscribed by Petersen at bottom of page 1: "For L. D. – / This ephemeral (scarcer than the Beer Broadside!) and utterly nonvaluable / (*not* the same as invaluable) record of an exhibit (pages 2 and 3) that took place / in ancient times in Gothic surroundings. Printed in permanent ink on fugitive / paper. Copy in the Massey Collection; copy (now) in the Brodsky. (I wonder / if Petersen has one.) / Put it in its ordered place. Carl."

433 Hoffman, Frederick J., and Olga W. Vickery, eds. *William Faulkner: Three Decades of Criticism*. East Lansing: Michigan State University Press, 1960. First edition, first printing, with dust jacket.

Inscribed on free front endpaper, in black ink, "For Louis Brodsky / Cleanth Brooks, Dec. 9, 1962"; on verso of half title, in blue ink, "Frederick J. Hoffman"; and on page 94 (first page of "Introduction to *The Portable Faulkner*"), in black ink, "For Louis Brodsky / Malcolm Cowley."

1 9 6 1

434 Letter from Phil Stone to Richard P. Adams, dated October 4, 1961, unsigned carbon typescript, 2 pages.

Concerns T. S. Eliot's influence on Faulkner.

435 Meriwether, James B. *The Literary Career of William Faulkner: A Bibliographical Study*. Princeton, New Jersey: Princeton University Library, 1961. First edition, first printing, with dust jacket.

Inscribed by Meriwether to Brodsky.

436 Meriwether, James B. *The Literary Career of William Faulkner: A Bibliographical Study*. Columbia, South Carolina: University of South Carolina Press, 1971. Authorized reissue of Princeton edition, second printing (1972), with dust jacket.

Inscribed by author on free front endpaper, in black ink: "This book, my first, / is inscribed to L. D. Brodsky, / who is the sort of person I / wrote it for, though I / didn't know him when I / did it / Memphis Airport / 6 Aug 77 / If this is useful to him / in forming his distinguished / collection, I am repaid / for the labor of making it." On title page, in black ink: "Jim Meriwether."

1 9 6 2

437 *Selected Short Stories of William Faulkner*.
New York: The Modern Library, 1962.
First edition, first printing, with dust jacket.

Modern Library edition (324).

438 "Hell Creek Crossing."

The Saturday Evening Post, 235 (March 31, 1962), 22–25.

Pre-publication excerpt from *The Reivers*.

439 "The Education of Lucius Priest."

Esquire, 57 (May 1962), 109ff.

Pre-publication excerpt from *The Reivers*.

440 Letter from Phil Stone to Richard P. Adams, dated June 1, 1962, unsigned carbon typescript, 2 pages.

Cites Balzac's influence on Faulkner and comments on *The Marble Faun, Soldiers' Pay, Mosquitoes,* and *A Green Bough*.

441 *The Reivers: A Reminiscence.*

New York: Random House, [June 4] 1962.
First edition, first printing, with original acetate dust jacket. The limited and trade copies of this book are from the same printing.

Number 451 of signed, limited issue of 500 copies.

442 *The Reivers: A Reminiscence.*

New York: Random House, 1962.
First edition, first printing, with dust jacket.

Presentation copy given to Emily and Phil Stone. On free front endpaper, in black ink:

> *To Emily and Phil*
> *from Bill*

On title page, in black ink:

> *William Faulkner*
> *Oxford Miss*
> *12 June 1962*

443 *The Reivers: A Reminiscence.*

New York: Random House, 1962.
First edition, first printing, with dust jacket.

Advance review copy, with slip laid in announcing date of publication as June 4, 1962.

444 *The Reivers: A Reminiscence.*

New York: Random House, 1962.
First edition, first printing, with dust jacket.

445 *The Reivers: A Reminiscence.*

New York: Random House, 1962.
First edition, first printing, with dust jacket.

  Book-of-the-Month Club edition, marked "W" and not "First Printing" on the copyright page. Jacket indicates "Book-of-the-Month Club Selection" and omits list price of $4.95 and date "6/62" from other first printing copies.

446 *The Reivers: A Reminiscence.*

New York: Random House, 1962.
First edition, first printing, with dust jacket.

  Jacket indicates "Book-of-the-Month Club Selection" but "First Printing" instead of "W" appears on the copyright page.
  Laid in is leaflet reprinting Clifton Fadiman's review from *Book-of-the-Month Club News*.

447 *Les larrons.*

Paris: Gallimard, 1964.
Trans. Maurice-Edgar Coindreau and Raymond Girard. Preface by Girard.
First French edition, with original glassine.

  Number 38 of limited issue of 67 copies on "vélin pur Lafuma-Navarre."

448 *Book-of-the-Month Club News*, June 1962. Includes cover photograph of Faulkner and promotional material on *The Reivers*, Book-of-the-Month Club selection for July 1962.

449 Letter from Phil Stone to Richard P. Adams, dated June 8, 1962, unsigned carbon typescript, 2 pages.

  Includes this postscript:

  Don't repeat this to anyone, but Bill has been home for a few days and I saw him on the street the other day. I have never seen him look so old before. It is not his eyes, but the skin around his eyes; looks like that of an old man, and he looks to me like he has aged about five years since I saw him a few months ago.

  Faulkner died less than a month later, on July 6, 1962.

450 Letter from Phil Stone to William Faulkner, dated June 13, 1962, unsigned carbon typescript, 1 page.

  Expresses appreciation for the autographed copy of *The Reivers* (see item **442**) which Faulkner left at Stone's law office the day before.

451 "Store Closing" broadside. Posted by business establishments in Oxford on the day of Faulkner's funeral, July 7, 1962. See plate 39.

Copy belonged to Phil Stone. Inscribed at bottom, in blue ball point, "Phil Stone."

With 10-by-13-inch manila envelope on which Stone has written, in black ball point: "Two Copies / of / Announcement of / closing of town for / Wm. Faulkner's / death— / One for Philip and / one for Araminta."

452 Letter from Phil Stone to Hubert Starr, dated July 11, 1962, unsigned carbon typescript, 1 page.

In response to Starr's letter of July 6. Expresses grief over Faulkner's death: "I had no idea that Bill's death would hit me as hard as it did but I have not gotten over it yet. . . Pardon this being so short but I still don't have a lot of pep for writing letters because of Bill."

453 *The Oxford Eagle*, Thursday, July 12, 1962.

First publication of the weekly *Eagle* following Faulkner's death on July 6. Contains numerous articles about Faulkner's death and life.

In Memory

of

William Faulkner

This Business Will Be

Closed

From 2:00 To 2:15 P.M.

Today, July 7, 1962

39 "Store Closing" broadside, signed by Phil Stone

V

BEYOND

1962 —

[Man] can't live forever. He knows that. But when he's gone somebody will know he was here for his short time. He can build a bridge and will be remembered for a day or two, a monument, for a day or two, but somehow the picture, the poem—that lasts a long time, a very long time, longer than anything.
—*Colloquy at Nagano Seminar*

V

BEYOND

Faulkner's death has in no way diminished the avalanche of publications devoted to his work. The annual bibliography of the Modern Language Association typically lists one hundred or more articles and books relating to Faulkner, and more doctoral dissertations (well over two hundred) have now been written on Faulkner than on any other American author. Only Shakespeare continues to outrank Faulkner as the subject of critical treatment by American literary scholars.

Yet there is still considerable work to be done. The posthumous publications of *The Wishing Tree* (1967), *Flags in the Dust* (1973), *Marionettes* (1975), and *Mayday* (1976), along with the bibliographical work of Carvel Collins, James Meriwether, and others, represent important steps in completing the Faulkner canon; but other materials, including some in the Brodsky Collection, remain unpublished. Joseph Blotner's monumental *Faulkner: A Biography* (1974) is an impressive and indispensable work yet already needs revision in light of information only recently made available.

Even Faulkner, who despite being a shy, reticent individual was always the supremely confident artist, would have to be impressed by the attention he continues to command nearly two decades after his death. Then again, maybe he would not be at all surprised. One recalls Faulkner's comment about the "longer view" of the writer who aims his work "not at Jones of 1957 but [at] Jones of 2057 or 4057." Again Faulkner remarked, "I think that a writer wants to make something that he knows that a hundred or two hundred or five hundred, a thousand years later will make people feel what they feel when they read Homer, or read Dickens or Balzac, Tolstoy, that that's probably his goal." Few critics, at least from this point in time, would doubt that Faulkner will join these other great writers in achieving that goal.

1962

454 *Faulkner's University Pieces*.

Tokyo: Kenkyusha Limited, 1962.
Comp. with introduction by Carvel Collins.
First edition, first printing, with dust jacket.

English text.
Inscribed by Collins to Brodsky.
Contains poems, essays, and drawings which Faulkner published from 1917 to 1925 in University of Mississippi publications *Ole Miss*, *The Mississippian*, and *The Scream*.

455 *William Faulkner: Early Prose and Poetry*.

Boston: Little, Brown and Company, [October 30] 1962.
Comp. with introduction by Carvel Collins.
First edition, first printing, with dust jacket.

Advance review copy. Laid in are review slip announcing publication date as October 30, 1962, and two reproductions from the book: a photograph of Faulkner in RAF uniform and a drawing by Faulkner of two dancers before a jazz band.
Expanded version of *Faulkner's University Pieces*.
Inscribed by Collins to Brodsky.

456 *William Faulkner: Early Prose and Poetry*.

Boston: Little, Brown and Company, 1962.
Comp. with introduction by Carvel Collins.
First edition, first printing, with dust jacket.

Advance review copy, with review slip laid in.
Inscribed by Collins to Brodsky.

457 *William Faulkner: Early Prose and Poetry*.

Boston: Little, Brown and Company, 1962.
Comp. with introduction by Carvel Collins.
First edition, first printing, with dust jacket.

Presentation copy given by Collins to Phil Stone. Inscribed on free front endpaper, in black ink: "To Phil, in gratitude / for the whole thing! / —Carvel."

458 *William Faulkner: Early Prose and Poetry*.

Boston: Little, Brown and Company, 1962.
Comp. with introduction by Carvel Collins.
First edition, first printing, with dust jacket.

Inscribed by Collins to Brodsky.

459 *William Faulkner: Early Prose and Poetry*.

Boston: Little, Brown and Company, 1962.
First edition, first printing, in paperback.

Atlantic-Little Brown Paperback (LB 1).
Inscribed by Collins to Brodsky.

460 *William Faulkner: Early Prose and Poetry*.

London: Jonathan Cape, 1963.

Beyond: 1962—

Comp. with introduction by Carvel Collins.
First British edition, first printing, in wrappers.

Advance review copy with printed label glued to front cover announcing publication date as November 1963.
Inscribed by Collins to Brodsky.

461 *William Faulkner: Early Prose and Poetry*.

London: Jonathan Cape, 1963.
Comp. with introduction by Carvel Collins.
First British edition, first printing, with dust jacket.

Inscribed by Collins to Brodsky.

462 *William Faulkner: Proses, poésies et essais critiques de jeunesse*.

Paris: Gallimard, 1966.
Ed. with introduction by Carvel Collins. Trans. with preface by Henri Thomas.
First French edition, first printing, in printed wrappers.

Number 1026 of limited issue of 1500 copies.
Inscribed by Collins to Brodsky.

1963

463 Faulkner, John. *My Brother Bill: An Affectionate Reminiscence*. New York: Trident Press, 1963. First edition, second printing, with dust jacket.

Copy belonged to Phil Stone. Inscribed on free front endpaper, in black ink: "Phil Stone / Thanksgiving 28th October 1963." Also signed on front flyleaf and half title page, in black ink: "Phil Stone."
Contains, in pencil, numerous annotations by Stone.

464 Thompson, Lawrance. *William Faulkner: An Introduction and Interpretation*. New York: Barnes & Noble, Inc., 1963. First edition, first printing, with dust jacket.

Inscribed by Thompson on free front endpaper, in blue ink: "Dear Louis Brodsky, / It please[s] me to / know that you have / this book in (or near) / your Faulkner collection. / Friendly regards / Lawrance Thompson."

1964

465 "A William Faulkner Exhibit: First, Limited, and Unusual Editions." Souvenir program for Brodsky exhibit at John M. Olin Library, Washington University, St. Louis, April 27–June 5, 1964.

466 Blotner, Joseph, comp. *William Faulkner's Library: A Catalogue.* Charlottesville: University Press of Virginia, 1964. First edition, first printing, with original tissue wrapper.

Inscribed by Blotner to Brodsky. On free front endpaper, in black ink: "To L. D. Brodsky, / who knows well many / of the books listed herein, / with best regards, / Joseph Blotner." On title page, in black ink: "Joseph Blotner / 6 Dec 1978."

1965

467 "A William Faulkner Exhibit." Souvenir program for Brodsky exhibit of first, limited, and unusual editions at St. Louis Public Library, February 1–28, 1965.

468 *The Marble Faun and A Green Bough.*
New York: Random House, [1965].
First Random House edition, first printing, with dust jacket.

Reprint of 1924 and 1933 volumes of Faulkner's poems, "reproduced photographically from copies of the original editions."

469 Stone, Emily Whitehurst. "How a Writer Finds His Material." *Harper's Magazine*, 231 (November 1965), 157–161.

Copy belonged to Emily Stone. Inscribed by her to Brodsky.
Discusses Faulkner's use of local sources and his relationship with Phil Stone.

470 Stone, Emily Whitehurst. "Faulkner Gets Started." *The Texas Quarterly*, 8 (Winter 1965), 142–148.

Copy belonged to Emily Stone. Inscribed on cover, "Emily W. Stone," and on p. 142, "To L. D. Brodsky, with respect and / affection ———— / August 23, 1977—Emily W. Stone."

471 Meriwether, James B., ed. *Essays, Speeches & Public Letters by William Faulkner.* New York: Random House, 1965. First edition, first printing, with dust jacket.

Inscribed by Meriwether to Brodsky.

472 Meriwether, James B., ed. *Essays, Speeches & Public Letters by William Faulkner.* London: Chatto & Windus, 1967. First British edition, first printing, with dust jacket.

Inscribed by Meriwether to Brodsky.

473 Webb, James W., and A. Wigfall Green, eds. *William Faulkner of Oxford.*

Beyond: 1962—

[Baton Rouge] Louisiana State University Press, 1965. First edition, first printing, with dust jacket.

Inscribed by Webb on half title page, in blue ink: "For / L. D. Brodsky / who has come to visit / Rowan Oak and Faulkner's / Yoknapatawpha. / James W. Webb / University, Mississippi / May 29, 1975."

1966

474 Warren, Robert Penn, ed. *Faulkner: A Collection of Critical Essays*. Englewood Cliffs, New Jersey: Prentice-Hall, Inc., 1966. First edition, first printing, with dust jacket.

Includes Malcolm Cowley's "Introduction to *The Portable Faulkner*," which is inscribed by Cowley to Brodsky.

475 Warren, Robert Penn, ed. *Faulkner: A Collection of Critical Essays*. Englewood Cliffs, New Jersey: Prentice-Hall, Inc., 1966. First edition, first printing, in paperback.

Spectrum paperback (S-TC-65).
Includes Malcolm Cowley's "Introduction to *The Portable Faulkner*," which is inscribed by Cowley to Brodsky.

476 Cowley, Malcolm. *The Faulkner-Cowley File: Letters and Memories, 1944–1962*. New York: The Viking Press, 1966. First edition, first printing, with dust jacket.

Inscribed by Cowley on half title page, in black ink: "Warmly inscribed for / L. D. Brodsky / Malcolm Cowley."
Recounts the story of the making of *The Portable Faulkner*, published in 1946.

477 Cowley, Malcolm. *The Faulkner-Cowley File: Letters and Memories, 1944–1962*. New York: The Viking Press, 1966. Viking Compass edition (C219), 1968, in paperback.

Inscribed by Cowley for Brodsky.

478 Cowley, Malcolm. *The Faulkner-Cowley File: Letters and Memories, 1944–1962*. London: Chatto & Windus, 1966. First edition, first British reprint, with dust jacket.

Inscribed on title page, in black ink: "The English edition too, / Malcolm Cowley."

479 Cowley, Malcolm. *The Faulkner-Cowley File: Letters and Memories, 1944–1962*. Tokyo: Fujiyama Publishers, 1968. Trans. Kenzaburo Ohashi and Kyoichi Harakawa. First Japanese edition, with dust jacket.

Copy belonged to Cowley. Inscribed on page 1 of the index, in Cowley's hand, in black ink: "For Louis Brodsky / —inscribed here in what / is, for Japanese, the / back of the book, / Malcolm Cowley."

1 9 6 7

480 *Lillabulero: Being a Periodical of Literature and the Arts*, 1 (Spring 1967), 18–29.

Reprints "Once Aboard the Lugger" (story) and "April," "Winter Is Gone," "Visions in Spring," "I Will Not Weep for Youth," and "A Child Looks from His Window" (poems) by Faulkner from *Contempo*, 1 and 2 (1932).

481 "The Wishing Tree."

The Saturday Evening Post, 240 (April 8, 1967), 48ff.

Complete text published three days before Random House edition.

482 *The Wishing Tree*.

New York: Random House, [April 11] 1967.
First edition, first printing, with dust jacket, boxed.

Number 21 of limited issue of 500 copies.
First book publication of child's story Faulkner wrote for a young friend in 1927.

483 *The Wishing Tree*.

New York: Random House, 1967.
First edition, first printing, with dust jacket.

Advance review copy, with slip laid in announcing publication date as April 24, 1967.
Publisher's note on page 85 (which is also printed on back flap of dust jacket) indicates 1967 publication, but copyright page lists 1964 and Library of Congress number shows [19]66. Actual publication date was April 11, 1967.
Front flap of jacket on this copy omits date "4/67," which is present on some copies.

484 *The Wishing Tree*.

New York: Random House, 1967.
First edition, first printing, with dust jacket.

Copy belonged to Emily Stone. Contains her interlinear collations, in red ink, with typescript version Faulkner had presented to Philip Stone in 1948. See item **264**.
Front flap of jacket lacking the date "4/67," present on some copies.

485 "L'Arbre aux Souhaits."

Beyond: 1962—

La Nouvelle Revue Français, No. 180 (December 1, 1967), 995–1022.
Trans. Maurice-Edgar Coindreau.

First appearance in French.

486 *L'arbre aux souhaits*.

Paris: Gallimard, 1969.
Trans. M.-E. Coindreau.
First French edition, first printing, with original glassine.

Number 20 of 41 copies on "vélin pur fil Lafuma-Navarre."

487 *Histoires diverses*.

Paris: Gallimard, 1967.
Trans. R.-N. Raimbault and Céline Zins.
First French edition, first printing, with original glassine.

Number 21 of limited issue of 42 copies on "vélin pur fil Lafuma-Navarre."
A collection of seventeen Faulkner short stories. Duplicates no other title.

1 9 6 8

488 "A Keepsake for the Occasion of a Lecture, 'William Faulkner: Man Working 1897–1962,' by Linton R. Massey." Gleeson Library Associates of the University of San Francisco, January 21, 1968.

Reproduces Faulkner's holograph letter to Ben Wasson, [n. d.], announcing Jill's birth and suggesting use of colored inks in printing of *The Sound and the Fury*.

489 Massey, Linton R., comp. *"Man Working," 1919–1962, William Faulkner: A Catalogue of the William Faulkner Collections at the University of Virginia*. Charlottesville: Bibliographical Society of the University of Virginia, 1968. Introduction by John Cook Wyllie. First edition, first printing.

490 Meriwether, James B., and Michael Millgate, eds. *Lion in the Garden: Interviews with William Faulkner 1926–1962*. New York: Random House, 1968. First edition, first printing, with dust jacket.

Inscribed by Meriwether to Brodsky.
Advance review copy with slip laid in announcing publication date as May 28, 1968.

491 Meriwether, James B., and Michael Millgate, eds. *Lion in the Garden: Interviews with William Faulkner 1926–1962*. New York: Random House, 1968. First edition, first printing, with dust jacket.

Inscribed by Meriwether to Brodsky.

1970

492 Meriwether, James B., ed. "Prefatory Note by Faulkner for His 'Appendix: Compson, 1699–1945.'" Trans. Maurice Edgar Coindreau.

Broadside reproducing last two paragraphs of essay subsequently published in *American Literature* (see item **494**).

Number 19 of "25 copies printed December 1970, as a Season's Greeting for friends of M. Coindreau and of the Pléiade Edition of Faulkner."

Inscribed, in black ink: "For L. D. Brodsky / Faulkner Collector / *par excellence* / with the / compliments of / the editor / (though not / the translator) / Jim Meriwether."

Also contains this note of explanation, in Meriwether's hand, in black ink: "These were / printed in / Versailles the / week before / Xmas 1970; / the publication / of the / translation / preceded by / almost 6 / months the / first / publi-/cation / in / English."

493 Emerson, O. B. "Faulkner and His Friend: An Interview with Emily W. Stone." *Comment*, 11 (Winter 1970–1971), 31–37.

Copy belonged to Emily Stone. Inscribed on cover, in red ink: "——— Emily Stone. / From O. B. / Emerson." Also inscribed on cover by Mrs. Stone to Brodsky.

1971

494 Meriwether, James B. "A Prefatory Note by Faulkner for the Compson Appendix." *American Literature*, 43 (May 1971), 281–284.

Inscribed on back cover, in pencil: "Prof Meriwether / Jim—Thought you / might want this / Matt [Bruccoli]." Also on back cover, in Meriwether's hand, in black ink: "Passed on to / L. D. Brodsky, / 12 Aug 77 / JBM."

Inscribed on page 281, in black ink: "James B Meriwether."

495 *Nobel Prize Library: William Faulkner, Eugene O'Neill, John Steinbeck*. New York: Alexis Gregory, and Del Mar, California: CRM Publishing, 1971. First edition, first printing.

Includes, in addition to selections by Faulkner, the Nobel Prize presentation address by Gustaf Hellström and "The Life and Works of William Faulkner" by Joseph Blotner.

Inscribed by Blotner, on half title page, in black ink, "For L. D. Brodsky, / a preeminent collector, / with best regards, / Joseph Blotner," and on page 105, also in black ink, "Joseph Blotner / 6 Dec 1978."

496 Katz, Joseph, ed. *Proof: The Yearbook of American Bibliographical and Textual Studies*. Vol. I. Columbia, South Carolina: University of South Carolina Press, 1971.

Beyond: 1962—

Includes "The Short Fiction of William Faulkner: A Bibliography" by James B. Meriwether.
Inscribed by Meriwether to Brodsky.

1972

497 Franklin, Malcolm A. "Pappy's Colored Family" and "Days and Nights in the Big Woods." *Mississippi Magazine*, 12 (Winter 1972), 7–8.

Headnote describes these items as excerpts from "the as yet unpublished book *Yoknapatawpha*" by Faulkner's stepson. Book was published in 1977 with alternate title, *Bitterweeds*.

1973

498 *Flags in the Dust.*

New York: Random House, [August] 1973.
Ed. with introduction by Douglas Day.
First edition, first printing, with dust jacket.

First publication of original, uncut version of novel published as *Sartoris* in 1929.

499 Katz, Joseph, ed. *Proof: The Yearbook of American Bibliographical and Textual Studies*. Vol. III. Columbia, South Carolina: University of South Carolina Press, 1973.

Includes "Faulkner's Correspondence with *Scribner's Magazine*" by James B. Meriwether.
Inscribed by Meriwether to Brodsky.

1974

500 Blotner, Joseph. *Faulkner: A Biography*. Corrected page proof which belonged to Blotner.

Inscribed by Blotner to Brodsky. On part title page, Book One, in black ink: "For L. D. Brodsky, / with pleasure that these / sheets have become a part / of his superb collection, and / with all best wishes, / Joseph Blotner / 9 January 1979."

501 Blotner, Joseph. *Faulkner: A Biography*. 2 vols. New York: Random House, 1974. First edition, first printing, boxed.

Volume I inscribed on front flyleaf, in black ink, "For L. D. Brodsky, / a devoted

Faulkner reader and discriminating / collector, / with best regards, / Joseph Blotner," and on title page, "Joseph Blotner / 6 Dec 1978."

Volume II inscribed on half title page, in black ink, "For L. D. Brodsky, / with best wishes, / Joseph Blotner," and on title page, "Joseph Blotner / 6 Dec. 1978."

502 Boozer, William. *William Faulkner's First Book: The Marble Faun Fifty Years Later*. Memphis: The Pigeon Roost Press, 1974. First edition, first printing, with dust jacket.

Number 224 of limited edition of 1000 copies.
Title page shows 1974; copyright page shows 1975.

503 Meriwether, James B., ed. A *Faulkner Miscellany*. Jackson: The University Press of Mississippi, 1974. First edition, first printing, with dust jacket.

Inscribed by Meriwether to Brodsky.

1 9 7 5

504 Meriwether, James B. "Blotner's Faulkner." *The Mississippi Quarterly*, 28 (Summer 1975), 353–369.

Inscribed by Meriwether to Brodsky.

505 *The Marionettes: A Play in One Act*.

[Charlottesville, Virginia] The Bibliographical Society of the University of Virginia and the University Press of Virginia, [1975].
First edition, first printing.

Unbound gatherings in slip case. Number 3 of 100 copies on Arches paper.
Facsimile edition of play Faulkner wrote and produced in six hand-lettered and -illustrated copies in 1920.
Accompanied by two promotional brochures.

506 *Marionettes: A Play in One Act*.

Oxford, Mississippi: The Yoknapatawpha Press, 1975.
First edition, first printing, boxed in brown case stamped in gold.

Facsimile edition of another copy (see item **505**) of play Faulkner hand-printed in 1920. Number 82 of limited edition of 510 copies, 500 of which were offered for sale, 10 of which (lettered A–J) were not for sale.
Accompanied by monograph by Ben Wasson entitled A *Memory of Marionettes*, in boards. Inscribed by Wasson.

507 Crane, Joan St. C., and Anne E. H. Freudenberg, comps. *Man Collecting: Manuscripts and Printed Works of William Faulkner in the University of Virginia Library*. Charlottesville: University Printing Office, 1975.

One of 900 unnumbered copies in illustrated paper wrappers—800 of which were distributed with original title page: this is one of the 800.

Published to accompany a Faulkner exhibit at the University of Virginia, November 16, 1975–January 31, 1976.

508 Crane, Joan St. C., and Anne E. H. Freudenberg, comps. *Man Collecting: Manuscripts and Printed Works of William Faulkner in the University of Virginia Library*. Charlottesville: University Printing Office, 1975.

On free front endpaper, in blue ink: "Inscribed for Louis Daniel Brodsky—/ For inclusion in his important private / collection of William Faulkner's works. / Joan St C Crane / [this is one of 16 copies out-of-series of the casebound / copies. It has the cancelled title page] 13 Dec. 1978." Also on free front endpaper, in black ink: "For Louis Daniel Brodsky— / Anne E. H. Freudenberg."

Annotation on free front endpaper, in red ink, reads: "corrected / 16 Nov. 1978 / J. St. C.C."

On colophon, in black ink: "1 of 16 out-of-series." Added, in blue ink: "presented to Louis Daniel Brodsky / JC."

Ten of the 16 out-of-series copies have the canceled title page.

509 Petersen, Carl. *Each in Its Ordered Place: A Faulkner Collector's Notebook*. Ann Arbor [Michigan]: Ardis Publishers, 1975. First edition, first printing, with dust jacket.

Inscribed by Petersen on title page, in blue ink: "Carl Petersen / For L. D. —/Whose Faulkner collecting / knows no slack season. / Carl / Farmington / Oct 1, 1977."

1976

510 "William Faulkner: An Exhibit." Brochure which accompanied an exhibit of first, limited, and unusual Faulkner editions from the collection of L. D. Brodsky, George N. Meissner Memorial Rare Book Department, Washington University Library, St. Louis, August 23–October 15, 1976.

511 *Mayday*.

[South Bend, Indiana] University of Notre Dame Press, 1976.
First edition, first printing, with slip case.

Facsimile edition of allegory which Faulkner hand-lettered and presented to Helen Baird in 1926.

Number 33 of limited edition of 125 numbered copies.

Accompanied by pamphlet, in wrappers, by Carvel Collins entitled *Faulkner's Mayday* (University of Notre Dame Press, 1977). Inscribed by Collins to Brodsky.

512 Blotner, Joseph, ed. *Selected Letters of William Faulkner*. Corrected galley proof (Random House edition) which belonged to the editor. Galleys 1–243, unbound.

Includes a number of letters deleted from the published book.
Inscribed by Blotner to Brodsky.

513 Blotner, Joseph, ed. *Selected Letters of William Faulkner*. Franklin Center, Pennsylvania: The Franklin Library, 1976. Limited first edition, first printing.

Inscribed by Blotner to Brodsky.

514 Blotner, Joseph, ed. *Selected Letters of William Faulkner*. New York: Random House, 1977. First trade edition, first printing, with dust jacket.

Advance review copy, with slip laid in announcing publication date as February 7, 1977.
Inscribed by Blotner to Brodsky.

515 Blotner, Joseph, ed. *Selected Letters of William Faulkner*. New York: Random House, 1977. First trade edition, first printing, with dust jacket.

Inscribed by Blotner to Brodsky.

516 Blotner, Joseph, ed. *Selected Letters of William Faulkner*. London: The Scholar Press, 1977. First British edition, first printing, with dust jacket.

Inscribed by Blotner to Brodsky.

517 Broach, Vance C. *Grande Dame: A Tribute to Bama Falkner McLean*. Privately printed monograph, 1976.

Contains numerous references to Faulkner's relationship with his Aunt 'Bama.
Inscribed by Broach to Brodsky.

518 Brown, Calvin S. *A Glossary of Faulkner's South*. New Haven: Yale University Press, 1976. First edition, first printing, with dust jacket.

Inscribed by Brown to Brodsky.

519 Wilde, Meta Carpenter, and Orin Borsten. *A Loving Gentleman: The Love Story of William Faulkner and Meta Carpenter*. Advance uncorrected galley proof. Galleys 1–259, in yellow printed wrappers bound with tape. Cover lists probable publication date as November 1976.

520 Wilde, Meta Carpenter, and Orin Borsten. *A Loving Gentleman: The Love Story of William Faulkner and Meta Carpenter*. New York: Simon and Schuster, 1976. First edition, first printing, with dust jacket.

Inscribed by both Wilde and Borsten to Brodsky.

521 Wilde, Meta Carpenter, and Orin Borsten. *A Loving Gentleman: The Love Story of William Faulkner and Meta Carpenter*. New York: Jove Publications, Inc., 1977. Paperback.

Beyond: 1962 —

522 Wolfe, George H., ed. *Faulkner: Fifty Years After The Marble Faun*. University, Alabama: The University of Alabama Press, 1976. First edition, first printing, with dust jacket.

Includes Joseph Blotner's essay, "The Sole Owner and Proprietor," which is inscribed by Blotner to Brodsky.

1 9 7 7

523 Keepsake from exhibit of Malcolm Franklin's Faulkner memorabilia, University of South Carolina, 1977.

Copies of two letters written by Franklin: one on the origin of *Bitterweeds*; the other, to Faulkner, from Europe on D-Day, June 6, 1944.
Number 11 of 100 xerox copies.

524 Franklin, Malcolm. *Bitterweeds: Life with Faulkner at Rowan Oak*. Irving, Texas: The Society for the Study of Traditional Culture, 1977. First edition, first printing, with dust jacket.

Number 75 of limited edition of 300 copies.
Inscribed on limitation page, in black ink: "Malcolm Franklin."

525 "William Faulkner's Letters to Malcolm Franklin." The appendix to *Bitterweeds*. Stapled, in cream colored wrappers.

One of 40 copies distributed in advance of publication of the book.

526 *Faulkner: Œuvres romanesques*.
Paris: Gallimard, 1977.
Introduction and notes by Michel Gresset.
First edition, first printing, with acetate dust jacket, boxed.

Contains earlier Gallimard translations of *Sartoris, The Sound and the Fury, Sanctuary,* and *As I Lay Dying*, plus the "Compson Appendix."
Inscribed on free front endpaper, in black ink: "M Gresset."

1 9 7 8

527 Wells, Lawrence, ed. *William Faulkner: The Cofield Collection*. Oxford, Mississippi: Yoknapatawpha Press, 1978. Introduction by Carvel Collins. First edition, first printing, with dust jacket.

Copy K of limited edition of 162 copies signed by J. R. Cofield and Jack Cofield, 150 of which were for sale and 12 of which (lettered A–L) were not for sale.
Inscribed by Wells to Brodsky.

528 Wells, Lawrence, ed. *William Faulkner: The Cofield Collection*. Oxford, Mississippi: Yoknapatawpha Press, 1978. Introduction by Carvel Collins. First edition, first printing, with dust jacket.

Number 150 of limited edition of 162 copies signed by J. R. Cofield and Jack Cofield, 150 of which were for sale and 12 of which (lettered A–L) were not for sale.
Limitation page in this copy tipped in upside down.
Laid in is matted 7-by-5-inch photograph of Faulkner made by J. R. Cofield. Signed: "Jack Cofield / 3/20/62" [the date of the photograph].
Inscribed by Wells to Brodsky.

529 Wells, Lawrence, ed. *William Faulkner: The Cofield Collection*. Oxford, Mississippi: Yoknapatawpha Press, 1978. Introduction by Carvel Collins. First edition, first printing, in printed wrappers.

Advance review copy.
Inscribed by Wells to Brodsky.

530 "Eunice."

The Mississippi Quarterly, 31 (Summer 1978), 449–452.

First publication of this early poem by Faulkner. See item **11j**.
Inscribed on page 449 by James B. Meriwether, the editor of the journal, in blue ball point: "With thanks for letting us / print 'Eunice' ——— / L. D. from Jim."
Also inscribed on contents page, in blue ball point: "James B Meriwether."

531 Provenance paper for Malcolm Cowley's personal, annotated copy of *The Portable Faulkner*, dated August 1978.

Traces history of the book. See plate 30.

532 Letter from Malcolm Cowley to L. D. Brodsky, dated August 15, 1978, signed ribbon typescript, 1 page.

Discusses the origin of the inscription which appears in the copy of *The Sound and the Fury* belonging to Cowley. See item **66** and plate 31.

533 Cowley, Malcolm. *—And I Worked at the Writer's Trade: Chapters of Literary History, 1918–1978*. New York: The Viking Press, 1978. First edition, first printing, with dust jacket.

Includes "Faulkner: The Etiology of His Art."
Inscribed on free front endpaper, in Cowley's hand, in black ink: "With cordial greetings to / Louis Brodsky / Malcolm Cowley / November 1978."

INDEX OF FAULKNER WORKS

Absalom, Absalom!, 3, 121, 155, 186–191, 428
"Ad Astra," 105, 111
"After Fifty Years," 17
"Afternoon of a Cow," 210, 254
"All the Dead Pilots," 111
"Ambuscade," 165, 193
"American Segregation and the World Crisis," 377
"Appendix: Compson, 1699–1945," 492, 494, 526
"Apres-Midi d'un Faune, L'," 15–17, 130
"April," 123i, 480
As I Lay Dying, 72–85, 252–253, 526
"Aubade," 11

"Ballade des Femmes Perdue, Une," 17
"Barn Burning," 206, 210
"Bear, The," 183, 229, 370–371, 405
"Bear Hunt, A," 371
"Beyond," 158
Big Woods, 370–375
"Black Music," 158
"Blackbird swung in the white rose tree, The," 11h
"Books and Things," 9n
"Boy and Eagle," 166

"Carcassonne," 9p, 111
"Cathay," 17
"Centaur in Brass," 126
"Child Looks from His Window, A," 132, 480
Collected Stories of William Faulkner, 274–279
"Courtesan Is Dead, The," 166
"Crevasse," 111

"Dead Dancer, A," 13c, 14–14d, 17
"Death Drag," 122, 158
"December: To Elise," 21k
"Delta Autumn," 230–231, 370

"Divorce in Naples," 111
"Doctor Martino," 119, 158
Doctor Martino and Other Stories, 71, 109–110, 119, 122, 129, 143, 145, 154–155, 158–162
Drawings, 8–8j, 10, 12–12d, 13a, 17, 184, 454
"Dry September," 86, 111
"Dying Gladiator," 26b, 130

"Education of Lucius Priest, The," 439
"Elder Watson in Heaven," 11, 11k
"Elly," 154, 158
"Episode," 348, 355, 369
"Error in Chemistry, An," 269
Essays, Speeches & Public Letters by William Faulkner, 471–472
"Eunice," 11j, 530

Fable, A, 9p, 333–340, 347, 368, 373
Faulkner in the University, 398, 424–427
Faulkner Reader, The, 331–332
Faulkner's University Pieces, 454–455
"Faun, The," 27b, 130
"Fire and the Hearth, The," 221, 225, 231
Flags in the Dust, 498
"Flowers That Died, The," 153
"Fool About a Horse," 185, 210
"Fox Hunt," 110, 158
Fragments (burned), 17–18

"Gallows, The," 21h, 147
"Go Down, Moses," 227, 231
Go Down, Moses, 9p, 183, 221, 223–225, 227, 229–239
"Gold Is Not Always," 225, 231
"Gray the Day," 21j, 147
Green Bough, A, 11a, 11d, 11f, 17, 21c–e, 21g–j, 21 1, 29, 123b–c, 123e, 123g–h, 147–152, 166, 440, 468
"Green Grow the Rushes O," 11g
"Green Is the Water," 166

Index

"Hair," 106, 111
Hamlet, The, 9p, 107, 109, 127, 185, 206, 208–220, 254, 381, 399, 400, 403
"Hand upon the Waters," 269
"He furrows the brown earth, doubly sweet," 21e, 147
"Hell Creek Crossing," 438
"Here He Stands," 166
Histoires diverses, 487
"Honor," 71, 158
"Hound, The," 109, 158, 210
"Hymn," 11

"I Decline to Accept the End of Man." *See* Nobel Prize Acceptance Speech
"I give the world to love you," 11e
"I Will Not Weep for Youth," 11i, 123a, 480
Idyll in the Desert, 121
"If There Be Grief," 21g, 123g, 166
"Indian Summer," 21c, 147
Indispensable Faulkner, The, 250
Intruder in the Dust, 3, 256–263, 266–267, 337

"Jail, The," 301
"Jealousy," 348, 355, 369
Jealousy and Episode, 369
Jefferson, Mississippi, 379
"Justice, A," 111

"Knew I Love Once," 123b
"Knight's Gambit," 269
Knight's Gambit, 129, 268–272

"Leg," 158
Light in August, 134–142
"Lilacs, The" (booklet), 17–18
"Lilacs, The" (poem), 12, 13–13c, 14d, 17, 29–30, 130, 147
"Lion," 183, 231
Lion in the Garden, 490–491
"Lizards in Jamshyd's Courtyard," 127, 210

"Man Comes, Man Goes," 152
Mansion, The, 409, 413–420, 422–423
Marble Faun, The, 18–18c, 21, 22–25, 28, 108, 120, 242b, 440, 468, 502, 522
"March," 21 1, 147
Marionettes, 9b, 11 1, 17, 505–506
Mayday, 9p, 17, 208, 511
"Mink Snopes," 423

"Mirror of Youth," 166
Mirrors of Chartres Street, 328–329, 355
Miss Zilphia Gant, 133
"Mississippi Hills: My Epitaph." *See* "My Epitaph"
"Mississippi Poems," 21–21 1
"Mistral," 111
"Monk," 269
"Moon of death, moon of bright despair," 21b
Mosquitoes, 43–49, 440
"Mother and Child," 166
"Mountain Victory, A," 143, 158
"Mule in the Yard," 164
"My Epitaph," 21g, 123g, 144, 147

"Name for the City, A," 281
"New Orleans," 26c, 130, 358
New Orleans Sketches, 26c, 348, 355–366
Nobel Prize Acceptance Speech, 286, 290, 295–300, 316, 319, 331
"Notes on a Horse Thief," 333, 347
Notes on a Horsethief, 282–283
"November 11th," 21j, 147

"O Atthis," 17
"Ode to the Louver," 31
"Odor of Verbena, An," 193
"Old Man," 331, 405
"Old Man Says, An," 11i
"Old People, The," 223, 231, 371
"On Criticism," 26a, 130
"On Privacy," 273, 367
"Once Aboard the Lugger," 123, 480
"Over the World's Rim," 21d, 147

"Pantaloon in Black," 224, 231
"Pastoral," 11
"Pierrot, Sitting Beside the Body of Colombine," 11, 11 1
"Poet Goes Blind, The," 21f
"Point of Law, A," 221, 231
Portable Faulkner, The, 66, 187, 243, 245–251, 265, 313–314, 324, 433, 474–476, 531
"Portrait," 19, 130
"Pregnancy," 21i, 147
Pylon, 167–181

"Race at Morning," 371
"Raid," 193
"Red Leaves," 111

Index

Reivers, The, 438–439, 441–448, 450
Requiem for a Nun (novel), 251, 281, 301–310, 312
Requiem for a Nun (play), 311
"Retreat," 193
"Riposte in Tertio," 193
"Rose for Emily, A," 70, 111, 128

Salmagundi, 16, 19–20, 26a–c, 27a–b, 29, 130–131
Sanctuary, 83, 89–103, 315, 526
"Sapphics," 17
Sartoris, 50–61, 498, 526
Selected Letters of William Faulkner, 512–516
Selected Short Stories of William Faulkner, 437
"Shall I recall this tree, when I am old," 21a
Sherwood Anderson & Other Famous Creoles, 38–42
"Skirmish at Sartoris," 182, 193
"Smoke," 129, 158, 269
Soldiers' Pay, 9p, 21j, 32–37, 440
Sound and the Fury, The, 62–68, 252–253, 331, 343–344, 488, 526, 532
"Spotted Horses," 107, 210, 405
"Spring," 123h
"Sun lay long upon the hills, The," 11a, 147

"That Evening Sun," 104, 111
"There Was a Queen," 145, 158
These 13, 70, 86, 104–106, 111–118
This Earth, 21g, 123g, 144
Three Famous Short Novels, 405–406

"To a Co-ed," 17
"To a Virgin," 123e
"To the Voters of Oxford," 280
"Tomorrow," 269
Town, The, 126, 164, 382–393
"Turn About," 158
"Turn again, Dick Whittington," 11c
"Twilight," 123c

"Unvanquished, The," 192–193
Unvanquished, The, 165, 182, 192–198, 421

"Vendée," 193
"Verse, Old and Nascent," 20, 27a, 130
"Victory," 111
"Visions in Spring," 123d, 480

"Waifs, The," 393
"Was," 231
"Wash," 155, 158
"When evening shadows grew around," 11d, 147
"When I rose up with morning," 11b
"When I was young and proud and gay," 11f, 147
"Wild Geese," 21d, 147
Wild Palms, The, 9p, 200–205
William Faulkner: Early Prose and Poetry, 16, 19–20, 26a–b, 27a–b, 455–462
"William Faulkner On Dialect," 398, 404
"Winter Is Gone," 123f, 480
"Wishing Tree, The," 264, 381, 484–485
Wishing Tree, The, 375, 481–483, 486
"Word to Virginians, A," 398

INDEX OF NAMES

Adams, Richard P., 434, 440, 449
Aiken, Conrad, 9
Aldington, Richard, 9b
Aldridge, John W., 324
Anderson, Sherwood, 9, 38–42

Babb, James T., 242h
Baird, Helen, 511
Balzac, Honoré de, 440
Barnett, Ned, 207
Barrett, C. Waller, 424
Bates, Arlo, 9i
Bell, Clive, 9e
Bizzarri, Edoardo, 251
Bloom, James, 394–395, 410
Blotner, Joseph, 4, 9, 9p, 11e, 163, 199, 222, 294, 323, 337, 398, 404, 407, 424–427, 466, 495, 500–501, 512–516, 522
Boozer, William, 502
Borsten, Orin, 184, 519–521
Bouchet, André du, 272
Bradford, Roark, 166
Braithwaite, William Stanley, 9c, 30
Breant, J., 392
Breant, L., 392
Breit, Harvey, 190
Brickell, Herschel, 166
Broach, Natalie Carter, 2
Broach, Vance Carter, 1, 2, 148, 201, 245, 252, 266, 517
Brodsky, Louis Daniel, 1, 11, 18, 147, 197, 241, 243, 248–251, 255, 265, 283, 312–315, 324, 334, 343, 352–353, 358, 360–366, 376, 396, 398, 404, 412–413, 422, 424–428, 431–433, 435–436, 454–456, 458–462, 464–467, 469–477, 479, 490–496, 499–501, 503–504, 508–518, 520–522, 527–530, 532–533
Brooks, Cleanth, 9a, 9c, 9p, 166, 433
Brown, Anna Robertson, 9k

Brown, Calvin S., 62, 166, 264
Brown, Mrs. Calvin S., 258
Brown, Calvin S., Jr., 518
Brown, Edith, 50, 166, 258
Bruccoli, Matthew, 494
Buzby, G. C., 108d

Cabell, James Branch, 9, 9p.
Campbell, Allan, 329
Camus, Albert, 310
Carpenter, Meta. *See* Wilde, Meta Carpenter
Carter, Hodding, 283
Carter, Katrina, 9, 9f–g, 9j–o, 9r–s
Chesterton, G. K., 9j
Cofield, J. R., 146, 199, 323, 527–529
Cofield, Jack, 527–528
Coindreau, Maurice-Edgar, 68, 83–85, 117–118, 142, 205, 310, 447, 485–486, 492
Collins, Carvel, 9p, 197, 273, 315, 343–344, 352, 358–366, 421, 454–462, 511, 527–529
Commins, Saxe, 326
Cooper, Monte, 28
Coughlan, Robert, 273, 318, 327, 345, 349–351
Courtin, Pierre, 84–85
Cowley, Malcolm, 57, 66, 136, 170, 187, 196, 234, 243–251, 255, 265, 273e, 312–314, 324, 334, 353, 370, 413, 422, 433, 474–479, 531–533
Cowley, Muriel, 234
Crane, Joan St. C., 507–508

Daniel, Robert W., 11, 240–242
Davis, Anne Louise, 399c–d
Dean, Leonard F., 296
Delgove, Henri, 60–61, 102–103
Demarest, Myrtle Ramey, 5–8, 10, 20–21, 24, 34, 52, 73, 77, 93, 135, 157, 168, 250, 261, 408

Index

Devine, Eric "Jim," 78, 115, 150, 260
Disney, Dorothy Cameron, 222
Dix, William S., 381
Doolittle, Hilda (H. D.), 9b
Downer, Alan S., 343
Dubramet, Jean, 48–49

Eades, Robbie, 6
Eliot, T. S., 434
Emerson, O. B., 493

Fadiman, Clifton, 446
Falkner, J. W. T., 23
Falkner, M. C., 13b–c, 14c–d
Falkner, Maud, 397
Falkner, W. C., 1–4
Faulkner, Alabama, 87–88, 112
Faulkner, Estelle Oldham, 112, 184, 199, 354
Faulkner, Jill. *See* Summers, Jill Faulkner
Faulkner, John, 9, 463
Faulkner, William, 3, 5–6, 9–9c, 9e, 9 1, 9p–q, 18, 69, 87–88, 146, 156, 163, 199, 207, 222, 226, 228, 240–242, 273, 284–286, 288, 291–294, 317–318, 320–323, 325–327, 330, 341–342, 345–346, 349–354, 368, 376, 378, 380–381, 394–402, 404, 407–412, 429–436, 449–453, 463–467, 469–470, 473–479, 488–489, 493, 495–497, 499–504, 507–510, 517–525, 527–529, 533. *See also* Index of Faulkner Works
Flaubert, Gustave, 9f
Fletcher, John Gould, 9b, 166
Flint, F. S., 9b
Ford, Ruth, 264, 311
Franklin, Malcolm, 60, 81, 184, 204, 216, 218, 222, 226, 257, 269, 275, 280, 317, 330, 346, 378, 384, 407, 416, 497, 523–525
Freudenberg, Anne E. H., 507–508

Gallimard, Pierre, 368
Gandon, Yves, 68
Gaucher, Maxime, 37
Giannitrapani, Angela Minissi, 429–430
Girard, Raymond, 447
Godfrey, Kenneth, 32
Gorky, Maxim, 9j

Green, A. Wigfall, 166, 473
Gresset, J., 427
Gresset, Michel, 526
Gwynn, Frederick L., 424–427

Hackett, E. Byrne, 108a
Hamblin, Robert W., 207
Harakawa, Kyoichi, 479
Hardy, Thomas, 9g
Harris, R. L., 5
Hawks, Howard, 282
Haxton, Kenneth, 283
Heckman, Albert, 144
Hellström, Gustaf, 495
Hergesheimer, Joseph, 9n
Herlihy, James Leo, 407
Hilleret, René, 219–220, 420, 427
Hirsch, L. D., 118
Hoffman, Frederick J., 313–314, 433
Hooton, Earnest Albert, 226
Housman, A. E., 11
Hughes, Richard, 36, 47, 67
Hurst, G. G., 8b, 8e, 8h
Huxley, Aldous, 9, 9q

James, Alice, 166
James, Henry, 9d, 9h

Katz, Joseph, 496, 499
Keats, John, 9, 9i
Kennon, Sykes, 156
Kreymborg, Alfred, 105

Lake, Estelle, 242f
Larbaud, Valery, 83
Lawrence, D. H., 9b
Lawson, Yves, 61
Leahy, Paul, 108b
Lincoln, Abraham, 8j
Loiseles, Norman Pierre, 102
Louis-Rousselet, G., 181
Lowell, Amy, 9b–c

McLean, 'Bama (Mrs. Walter B.), 1, 3, 11, 11 1, 43, 64, 87–88, 94, 112, 146, 148, 199, 233, 242e, 242g–h, 266, 287–288, 304, 372, 421, 517
MacLeish, Archibald, 124–125
McMillin, Marguerite, 285

Index

Malcheski, Henry, 108c
Malraux, André, 102–103
Masefield, John, 9m, 9o, 9s
Massey, Linton R., 488–489
Mayfield, Walter B., 69
Mays, Benjamin E., 377
Meissner, George N., 510
Mencken, H. L., 31
Meriwether, James B., 9, 380, 394–396, 410–412, 431, 435–436, 471–472, 490–492, 494, 496, 499, 503–504, 530
Miller, Llewellyn, 349
Millgate, Michael, 9 1, 490–491
Miner, Ward, 320, 325
Mohrt, Michel, 368, 379
Mumford, Lewis, 105

Nishizaki, Ichiro, 355–357
Noble, William, 407

Ober, Harold, 399
O'Brien, Fred, 25
O'Donnell, George Marion, 212
Ohaski, Kenzaburo, 479
Oldham, Mrs. Lemuel, 11h
Olin, John M., 465

Parks, Joe, 23
Petersen, Carl, 432, 509
Peyre, Henri, 376
Pimental, Osmar, 346

Queneau, Raymond, 48–49
Quiller-Couch, Arthur, 9a

Raimbault, R. N., 60–61, 102–103, 117–118, 151, 162, 181, 191, 198, 239, 263, 340, 487
Ramey, Myrtle. *See* Demarest, Myrtle Ramey
Reed, W. M. ("Mac"), 168
Roberts, H. Wilson, 146
Rosenfeld, Paul, 105
Rovere, Richard H., 141
Russell, Bertrand, 284

Sassoon, Siegfried, 9 1
Saxon, Lyle, 166
Sewall, Richard B., 428
Shelley, Percy Bysshe, 20

Shirazi, J. M., 9j
"Simms, Ernest V.," 31
Sims, Cecil, 377
Smith, Harrison, 295
Smith, Henry Nash, 133
Somerville, Ella, 156
Spenser, Edmund, 20
Spratling, William, 38–42
Starr, Hubert ("Herb"), 33, 44, 53, 63, 74, 89, 131, 159, 169, 359, 452
Stevens, Wallace, 9c
Stone, Araminta, 256, 270, 274, 303, 451
Stone, Emily Whitehurst, 9e, 97, 156, 166, 211, 228, 256, 270, 274, 278, 442, 469–470, 483, 493
Stone, James, 291, 341, 400
Stone, Phil, 3, 9, 9a–e, 9g–s, 17–18, 21, 21h, 24, 31, 69, 72, 97, 108, 120, 134, 156, 163, 191, 207, 211, 228, 232, 240, 242b–d, 244, 247, 256, 267, 270, 273–274, 278, 282, 291, 303, 318, 320–323, 336, 344–345, 371, 380–381, 383, 397, 399, 411, 415, 429–430, 434, 440, 442, 449–452, 457, 463
Stone, Philip Alston, 208, 256, 264, 270, 274, 303, 408, 430, 451, 483
Stricklin, H. W., 1
Summers, Jill Faulkner, 287–288, 354, 488
Swinburne, Algernon, 9, 11

Tate, Allen, 166, 255
Tate, Caroline, 166
Thompson, Lawrance, 464
Thurmond, Richard J., 1
Till, Emmett, 378
Titzell, Josiah, 38
Tolson, Melvin B., 317, 330, 378
"Trueblood, Ernest V.," 254

Vickery, Olga W., 313–314, 433
Vorce, Ch.-P., 117–118, 162, 191, 198

Warren, Robert Penn, 166, 474–475
Wasson, Ben, 10, 283, 488, 506
Wasson, Ben F., Sr., 11 1, 242a
Webb, James W., 473
Wells, Lawrence, 527–529
Wells, Oliver, 124–125
West, Rebecca, 9d

Index

Whitehurst, Emily. *See* Stone, Emily Whitehurst
Whittington, Dick, 11c
Wilde, Meta Carpenter, 184, 519–521
Wiley, Bell I., 377
Wilkins, Holland, 88
Wolfe, George H., 522

Wright, Ella, 8j
Wright, Willard Huntington, 9e
Wylie, Elinor, 9r
Wyllie, John Cook, 489

Zins, Céline, 487